# Kayla Ihrig

# HOW TO BE A DIGITAL NOMAD

Build a successful career while travelling around the world

KoganPage

First published in Great Britain and the United States in 2024 by Kogan Page Limited

2nd Floor, 45 Gee Street
London
EC1V 3RS
United Kingdom
www.koganpage.com

8 W 38th Street, Suite 902
New York, NY 10018
USA

4737/23 Ansari Road
Daryaganj
New Delhi 110002
India

© Kayla Ihrig 2024
The right of Kayla Ihrig to be identified as the authors of this work has been asserted by her in accordance with the Copyright, Designs and Patents Act 1988.

**ISBNs**
Hardback    9781398613119
Paperback   9781398613058
Ebook       9781398613102

**British Library Cataloguing-in-Publication Data**
A CIP record for this book is available from the British Library.

**Library of Congress Cataloging-in-Publication Data**
Names: Ihrig, Kayla, author.
Title: How to be a digital nomad : build a successful career while travelling the world / Kayla Ihrig.
Description: London, United Kingdom ; New York, NY : Kogan Page, [2024] | Includes bibliographical references and index.
Identifiers: LCCN 2023048922 | ISBN 9781398613058 (paperback) | ISBN 9781398613119 (hardback) | ISBN 9781398613102 (ebook)
Subjects: LCSH: Telecommuting. | Travelers--Employment. | Travel--Computer network resources. | Vocational guidance. | Work-life balance.
Classification: LCC HD2336.3 .I57 2024 | DDC 331.25/68--dc23/eng/20231026
LC record available at https://lccn.loc.gov/2023048922

Typeset by Hong Kong FIVE Workshop, Hong Kong

*To my husband Bert-Jan Schilthuis,*
*parents Lori and Bruce Ihrig,*
*and sister Julia Gray.*

*To mom, dad and Julie: I owe so much of my joy*
*to you three for supporting all of my aspirations*
*in life in countless emotional and tangible ways,*
*even when my plans kept you up at night (sorry).*

*To Bert-Jan: you are the greatest gift that travel*
*brought me. The marvel of everywhere we've*
*gone and everything we've seen comes second to*
*the miracle that we get to live our lives together.*

*I will never be able to fully articulate the gifts*
*you've all given me. This book and the*
*experiences it represents would not exist without*
*you all. How I got so lucky, I'll never know.*

# Contents

# About the author

Kayla Ihrig bought a one-way ticket out of the United States in 2017 and has spent most of her time abroad since. Inspired by remote workers online and the feeling that life was passing her by at her nine-to-five, she found work online and fumbled her way through an attempt at executing the exact life she wanted. Years abroad have manifested lasting friendships and the typical highs and lows of the travel lifestyle, from unexpected adventures and once-in-a-lifetime experiences to dealing with technology malfunctions and health issues through Google Translate. Her insights, stories and interviews help aspiring digital nomads believe in and execute the best-case scenario version of their careers.

# Acknowledgements

Thank you to the people who supported me as I wrote: Bert-Jan Schilthuis, Lori and Bruce Ihrig, Julia and Aaron Gray, Lien and Harry Schilthuis, Kelley Leung, Susan Hin-Koncelik, and Matt James.

Thank you to the travellers and experts who contributed stories and advice: Kat Smith (www.findaway broad.com), Travis and Heather Sherry (https://extrapackof-peanuts.com), Jason Moore (https://zerototravel.com), Kaycee Bowen and the extended Location Indie team (https:// locationindie.com), Steven K Roberts (https://microship. com), Krystal and Eric Nagle (www.naglemediacompany. com), Gabe Marusca (www.gabemarusca.com), Emily Szopinski, Mitko Karshovski (www.remoteinsider.xyz), Mikaela Donelan, Nic Bartlett (https://weareeleanor.com), Nadalie Bardo (https://itsallyouboo.com), Kelly Carbone, Rob Palmer (https://robpalmer.com), Sam Palmer, Rachel and Sasha Story (www.gratefulgnomads.com), Lynne Lessard (www.travelynne.ca), Zoe Ashbridge (www.forank.com), Jessie van Breugel (www.thecreatoracademy.xyz), Hanna Larsson (https://hannalarsson.me), Kaila Dalgleish (https:// girlsguidetolivingabroad.substack.com) and Tim Beck (www. computermedixinc.com).

Thank you to Jeff Raykes, Barb Hauge and Jerry Richardson for all the formative conversations, mentorship and friendship in my early career.

Thank you to the educators who helped me love writing: David Loomis, Michele Papakie and Mr Fleckenstein.

Thank you to Rachel Cargle and Annie Carter for encouraging me to travel. The jump I took to go abroad in 2017 directly stemmed from our chance meeting at that hostel in Phoenix.

Thank you to every traveller with whom I've shared stories and laughs over the years.

# Introduction

# So, you want to be a digital nomad?

There's a phenomenal hitch in time that you've brushed up against in your life: it's the feeling that every experience takes longer the *first* time you encounter it. Time slows down on your first day driving to a new job or shopping in a new supermarket. The second pass at each of these tasks is mentally expedited. The mind switches to autopilot mode quickly and quietly, leaving a vague half-thought in the back of your mind: '*This felt so much longer on the way there.*' On these maiden journeys, you're more engaged with life.

This phenomenon is no accident and there's a simple equation behind it. If you want to slow the rate at which sand slips through life's hourglass, have as many new experiences as possible. There are potentially many ways to achieve this result, but one of the grandest answers is travel.

Restless feet have always turned to the road when grappling with how we spend our finite amount of time, but that life of wandering would force us to diverge from society at many points. Maintaining a career, relationships and a silhouette of normality was elusive. While travellers who wish to quietly disappear into the currents of the world are still free to do so, it's no longer necessitated by the journey. Income is now as mobile as we are, whether that be a salaried remote role or freelance opportunities with clients from around the globe. With a laptop and a WiFi connection, travellers now have access to their careers, relationships and familiar comforts from anywhere in the world. This is the age of the digital nomad.

While we may be taking a road that society sees as less travelled, digital nomads are treading a well-laid path set by travellers over millennia. We do, however, find ourselves in the unique position of being able to explore the world with our career, income and relationships in tow. How lucky are we to be alive right now? Whether it be through salaried positions or self-employment, aspiring travellers will read on the coming pages how travel works as a digital nomad, how to make a plan for themselves and how to thrive abroad, even through life's curveballs.

You've found a portal into a life where you can have endless experiences that summon you to awareness. Here's how to walk through it.

## Why we travel

*'Your life is better than your best dream for it.'*

JASON RUSSELL

A school bus turned the bend and started winding its way towards us. Not a normal school bus, though. It looked like it had driven straight out of a fever dream: brightly coloured with a roof rack full of packages, it barrelled towards us at a quick pace. Too quick, in fact, to stop in time to pick us up. I stood there squinting through the bright sunlight, wearing a huge stuffed backpack on my back and a smaller backpack on my front, at each elbow a fellow traveller I'd met the day before.

Suddenly, a short, tanned man hung out of the bus's door on one arm and yelled, 'Where are you going?' in Spanish. We yelled back: 'Atitlán!' '*Vámonos!*' he shouted, waving us onto the bus. He pulled himself back from the steps and the bus decelerated, but not completely. While this bus might have been making a metaphorical stop to pick us up, it clearly wouldn't be coming to a physical halt.

I didn't fully understand what was happening. A month earlier in my normal life in Chicago, if ever uncertain about catching a bus I would have just stepped back and waited for the next one. Although the next brightly coloured Guatemalan bus would come, I wouldn't have any more information than I did now. I had been begging life to give me an adventure and here it was, in the form of a hot, barrelling, wildly painted chunk of metal. Without saying a word, we all started jogging alongside the bus and jumped onto the open steps, pulling ourselves up one by one.

Eyes wide. Heart pounding. Mind rushing. The entire event probably only lasted from 10.23 to 10.24 on this Tuesday morning, but it was a moment that's foundational to the experience of being a digital nomad. Travellers often summarize it using the same three words: '*why we travel*'. The magnetic pull of finding yourself in unfamiliar places, solving unfamiliar problems, experiencing unfamiliar joys is extraordinary. It's why many digital nomads set out to travel long term, with the dream of reliable income being realized through technology. The desire to extend travel as long as possible isn't new and we now have unprecedented access to tools and a surprisingly uncomplicated path to facilitate the journey.

## Who is digital nomadism for?

Digital nomadism is for normal people. You don't need to be a more fit, stylish, adventurous or worldly version of yourself before you're ready to work from anywhere. You don't have to look a certain way in a bathing suit, become ten years younger or buy a new wardrobe. I fear it's only a matter of time before a reality TV host with a microphone approaches me in the street and asks if they can restyle me for an episode of their show. Yet I'm still allowed in the club.

You look like a digital nomad the way you are now. Any sense of worldliness and travel expertise that you feel you might lack now will come with time, though you might have to learn some things the hard or funny way. Don't worry, it's survivable. I once had an entire enthralled conversation with someone about their trip to Serbia having confused it with Siberia. No one asked to see my credentials or questioned how someone so unsavvy was allowed to pass through so many customs checkpoints.

The prerequisites for anyone who wants to be a digital nomad are simple: you must learn how to generate income online and have the desire and ability to travel. Where you go and how long you stay away for don't matter; at least they don't matter to me. In the most technical sense, the term digital nomad applies only to truly nomadic people: individuals with no home address or permanent dwelling, who drift around while supporting themselves online. But digital nomadism is only about travel on the micro level. Zoom out and you'll find that the real opportunity at stake is intentional choice.

If you gathered a group of 100 digital nomads in a room and asked them about the things remote work has afforded them, you wouldn't hear just about travel. You'd hear stories about people becoming temporary caretakers for family members. Tales of moving for love and making decisions that represent the best interests of their spouse and kids. You might also be surprised to see a group of people who are different in age, family type, travel style and everything else. Remote work and a love of travel aren't bound by any set of stereotypes.

All demographic factors vary and they should: the skills required by this lifestyle aren't special and the labels don't matter. I hope that you'll join in my permitting flexibility and throwing any prestige of super-minimalism or ultra-traveller status out the window. The umbrella of digital nomadism has expanded and there's room for all of us. It isn't a members-only club; there's no podium at the end with medals for the winners who have accumulated the most passport stamps or gone the longest without having an electricity bill to pay.

Those who gauge their experience using these metrics are missing, frankly, the entire point of this lifestyle: the independence to go where you see fit. The digital nomad lifestyle isn't about travelling alone, it's about the choice to get an infinitely higher number of opportunities out of your life.

People who secure the skills to provide for themselves online will find themselves deeper inside of life than they could've been at a desk. Yes, the ability to work from anywhere will take you to the mountain tops. It might also take you to your friend's side while they undergo cancer treatment. You'll journey to cheer up family members who need a distraction from a tough time. You'll find yourself saying yes to invitations and offers that you never could have committed to with a nine-to-five desk job. The profound flexibility to work from anywhere is going to change everything about how you make decisions in your life.

While there's no superiority to the different labels of the lifestyle, it is helpful to understand the differences between the terms. Jobs where you must physically show up to work every day in a predetermined location are called **location-dependent jobs**. The inverse is a **location-independent job**, which is what digital nomads have. Many location-dependent jobs are nine-to-five or desk jobs, but some people may be working part-time or doing shift work.

From here forward, let's refer to having a location-dependent job as 'normal life'. It's a neutral statement, with no negativity attached. In fact, let's agree right now to never speak negatively about normal life. We'll never call it the 'matrix' or say that anyone who likes normal life is ignorant to the opportunity of location independence. This opportunity should be spoken about in humble, unpretentious tones. Digital nomadism is a privilege and one should never throw their privilege around, fraudulently claiming philosophical high ground over others. It's ignorant and it's also oblivious to the fact that many digital nomads will end up back in normal life. A version of it, at least. Perhaps they will work online forever, but they'll buy homes, grow gardens and pursue all matters of a fixed, stationary life.

Hence, we will never beat up on normal life; we will simply discuss what you lose and what you gain when you leave it behind. And yes, there are losses. While becoming a digital nomad may make your dreams come true, like everything in life it comes at a price, as you'll see in the coming chapters. Should you choose to forgo Monday to Friday for yesterday, today and tomorrow, your interpretation of what's possible will never be the same. You will find yourself in unexpected places, surrounded by unexpected people, solving problems that you previously would have sworn you couldn't navigate. It might just be one of the great adventures of your life.

## My story

My name's Kayla and I would like to be your friend who works online and travels. When you feel doubt or face slowdowns or pushback from the process, reach for the reminder that you have a friend who did it too. A friend who went through the whole process, came *very* close to chickening out, but ultimately became a digital nomad despite being terrified. I'm standing on the other side of this chasm of decisions and planning and leaps of faith with a big smile, waving with both arms. If this chasm crossing was in the physical world, you'd land on the other side and I'd immediately take you to a cafe for a baked good where you could fill me in on all the details.

Realizing that I had no friends who worked online and travelled in real life, I turned to Instagram and Facebook groups for shared enthusiasm and encouragement in 2016. I was living in Chicago, with a job that I had described as my dream job not even 12 months earlier. The job itself wasn't bad and frankly nothing about my life was bad either. I was living alone (a recent wealth milestone), working downtown, making more than enough money to live and have some fun in the process. To any rational person, this was a situation to maintain. But the pros of my job simply could not justify the cost of dictating where I spent 50 weeks of the year.

Whole weeks and months could fly off the calendar like a movie montage illustrating the passage of time, yet the time itself was slipping by with an air of distinct insignificance.

There was a nagging vacuum in my life that slowly took over more and more real estate of my daily thoughts: *wasn't life supposed to be more fun?*

I became consumed with this question. On 19 October 2016 I wrote in a notebook, 'Maybe it's not such a crisis. But maybe it is.' A few days later, on the next page, after non-stop pondering, I conclusively scribbled, 'I don't have any excuses for not being who I want to be.' In search of perspective, I began asking colleagues if they thought their lives were fun. A median answer quickly emerged: life theoretically *ought* to be fun, but that's not reality.

My self-diagnosis was that I was sleepwalking through life and despite having done no solo international travel, I was convinced that travelling was the cure. So after work each day I escaped into a different reality: podcasts, social media accounts, blog posts and documentaries about travel. I was entranced by these people and the places they'd been. Hearing their stories felt like looking up at mountains of accomplishment. I developed a motto: if they could, I can. *Right? Right.* My need for self-assurance was constant. I changed my phone background to display whatever rallying inspiration I needed that week and hung Post-it notes with encouragement around my apartment. To an outsider, it probably looked like a Pinterest board had thrown up on my life.

In the spring of 2017, it was decided: I would start in Mexico and then I would tackle the world. With a loose plan in place, I bought the big backpack that would carry all my stuff and propped it up against the wall across from my bed. It was a consistent force gazing at me daily and as the weeks passed and the air outside warmed, it started to win the staring contest with my nervousness. I stuck a Post-it note on the wall next to the backpack that said, *'Don't be scared.'*

Then one day, wondering if I was making a big mistake, I moved the backpack over a few inches to cover up the Post-it note. My steadfastness was waning; it was holding up the mirror of my fear too closely. I hadn't handed in my notice at work yet, I surely didn't have the skills needed and I had moved into my apartment not even a year ago. I genuinely enjoyed most aspects of my job, yet here I was thinking of trading in a comfy salary for a week-to-week freelance writing gig covering topics I didn't even like. *Maybe some dreams are too big to actually achieve?* I started wondering.

My uncertainty kept me up at night. As your new friend, there's something I really want you to hear: when it comes to travel, fear is not a barrier to entry. It might even be a prerequisite. We can do the secret handshake when you get here. At the meeting with my boss to give my notice, I was sweating so badly that the bottoms of my glasses that rested on my cheeks fogged up. It's embarrassing to pretend to confidently deliver news when your physical appearance is undermining that confidence so visibly, but all that matters is that it's done.

At weak moments, after I'd pulled the trigger and resigned from my job, the digital nomad lifestyle felt like something that I had inflicted on myself and therefore *had* to see through. That was to my benefit, though, because the greatest force propelling me forward was the certainty that I'd regret grounding my plans when I was already this far down the runway.

Travelling, and not kicking my aspirations down the road, was the best decision I ever could have made for myself. Because of remote work, I have found myself in the oddest of places: in Montenegro sharing a glass of homemade alcohol over breakfast with an Airbnb host who spoke a language I didn't understand; walking through train terminals vibrating with the chants of Hungarian soccer fans on their way to an afternoon match; dancing in a crowd of singing Croatian concert goers beneath clear night skies and palm trees.

It hasn't been without problems – in the coming pages I'll share stories of poor health, tech breakdowns and travel failures galore and how you can avoid some of them yourself. The mistakes, mishaps and minefields of my experience will be your roadmap, but there's something you have to do on your own: accept that you stand at a fork in the road leading two ways. On the right is the risk of trying to become a digital nomad and failing or having a bad experience. On the left is the risk of staying at home and deferring your travel plans in the hopes that you will have the ability, money and gumption to do it later. That will work out fine for some people, but time and money are never guaranteed and gumption rarely shows up on its own without being summoned.

I don't know your exact situation, but I do know that there are digital nomads with families, of different nationalities, with all levels of travel experience and of varying degrees of education who have managed to get what they want out of their careers and bucket lists. I can't help but believe that you're capable of that same transition. In fact, metamorphic transitions are not nearly as uncommon as you think.

### Big transitions

The car's creaky door screeched shut next to me and I stared out over the dashboard. This was a new experience. A friend had lent me her small vehicle for a few months. It was time to drive it back home through the flat farmland of the provincial Netherlands where I was now living, and I wasn't alone. A tall man with short but untamed curly hair sat behind the wheel. With a twinkle in his eye and a dimple-revealing smile, he turned his head and said, 'We could drive all the way to China, you know.'

Meet Bert-Jan (pronounced *beart-yon*), a happy, day-dreaming, flip-flop-wearing Dutch man who became my travel partner in 2017 and my husband in 2019. We met in Guatemala while he was on a six-month backpacking trip, pondering whether he would remain a high school teacher for the rest of his life. The answer, as it turned out, was no. Bert-Jan was the first person I ever turned into a digital nomad and let me just say that it was *quite* the U-turn. When I moved into Bert-Jan's apartment, he didn't have WiFi, had never owned a laptop and had never been on a video call. And maybe an even more profound chasm to cross was how he spent his time. Bert-Jan's life was in the physical world: he commanded a classroom by day and played guitar and read books by night. He spent very little time online and sitting at a computer all day was, to him, the worst-case scenario in life. *Until* he realized the daydream of uncapped travel as a digital nomad.

He already had the travel part down. Possessing the rarest of qualities, Bert-Jan is universally easy to love. He loves life and life loves him right back. In Dutch, they call this being a *zondagskind*, which translates to 'Sunday child'. It means that things tend to go your way. That quality is never more apparent than when Bert-Jan is abroad; it comes effortlessly to him. Not just the action of travelling, but the ease and the joy of being detached from normal life. I remember it vividly from the first day that we met in Spanish school. He was shocked, even appalled, that I had brought my work along with me backpacking. When I asked him about his work, he stood barefoot before me, with the sincerest of smiles, glowing as he said, 'I don't have to read a single email for six months.' Being a remote worker was a journey that took much more effort, but he learned. First he learned to do it and then he learned to love it. Because of all the ways to travel, travelling as a digital nomad is one of the grandest.

## Why travel as a digital nomad?

It was a Friday afternoon and with the essential work for the week already in the bag, Travis and Heather Sherry decided to spontaneously go out for lunch. Donning flip-flops and t-shirts, they had settled into a sushi restaurant when a clowder of men walked through the door, clearly on an out-of-office Friday lunch. They were wearing polo shirts and khakis for casual Friday (a staple in some American workplaces where employees are allowed to dress down once a week), with big smiles on their faces, talking about how nice it was to be out of the office in the middle of the day. Travis realized he hadn't worn a polo shirt in seven years. To these guys, being out of the office on a Friday afternoon was freedom, but to Travis, that was the exact opposite.

Ask most digital nomads why they live this lifestyle and you'll get a long-winded answer detailing places they've been, experiences they've had and bucket list destinations on the horizon. But not Travis. He can sum up his 'why' in four words: the Triangle of Freedom.

This catchy ethos wasn't born overnight; at first, there was just one point: location freedom. It was this precise siren's call that led Travis and his wife Heather away from their desks as English teachers and down the road of remote work in 2012. For years, they explored the world as travel bloggers and podcasters on a seemingly endless supply of energy for travel. Then, a point came where it wasn't fun to take Zoom calls at 1 am from the other side of the world anymore. More than just the freedom to be *where* they wanted, they also wanted to determine *when*. Time freedom was added to their list of musts. And after years of blogging, running a membership and investing in real estate, among other income streams, they realized the final point of the triangle: financial freedom. Having control and flexibility over how they made money was just as valuable as the other pieces of the puzzle.

While this list of demands feels out of pace with society's normal measuring stick, Travis was certain he wasn't alone in his steadfast pursuit of them. Along with travel blogger and entrepreneur Jason Moore, Travis co-founded a paid community for people interested in pursuing the Triangle of Freedom together called Location Indie (short for location independence). They didn't want the values and dreams of this lifestyle to feel abstract to others, so they created a space where remote workers (or aspiring ones) could find each other, learn skills, virtually co-work and more. The community has been going strong since 2014 and housed thousands of members; their podcast, Location Indie, has impacted even more people.

The podcast was precisely how I found Travis and Jason. Listening to it on my way to and from work became a lifeline between my current disposition and the dream I had for my life. I would settle into my seat on the bus after a long day of work in Chicago and hear those familiar words: '*Welcome to the Location Indie podcast! A behind-the-scenes, unfiltered, no-holds-barred look at realities of the location-independent lifestyle from two guys who are living that lifestyle.*' The episodes could centre around anything: the annoyance of filing taxes, the joy of recording a podcast from a gorgeous exotic destination, skills, challenges or anything else.

The podcast began in 2016 and while the conversation is still centred around location independence, today it explores wider themes. For Travis, the freedom to drop his kids off at school every day is just as important as his ability to work from anywhere. 'Taking away those simple moments would be as devastating as taking away the ability to travel,' he said. Travis's trajectory with the digital nomad lifestyle matches that of countless other remote workers that I interviewed:

- Discover the ability to make your travel dreams a reality.

- Successfully execute the plan and achieve your goals.

- Apply to the next aspiration waiting in the wings.

The greatest gift of this lifestyle is the fact that the Triangle of Freedom will go with you anywhere in life, far beyond travelling. Digital nomadism is a vehicle for pursuing the exact life that you want. It doesn't have to be rooted in travel forever, nor does it have to be a profound or enlightened quest. You don't need to be taking a close look at the universe and trying to unravel its secrets. The justification for travel can be as simple as wanting to see things for yourself.

This is a safe space to say that life feels like a whistle and you want it to feel like a symphony. Digital nomadism can be that portal for you. Evenings and weekends can be spent getting lost down winding streets, listening to live music that you don't understand a single word of or on bus rides to completely unknown destinations. Work can be done from an Airbnb on an island in the Mediterranean, a moving car road-tripping across Australia or an airport in Jakarta.

For the travel-hearted, this opportunity is everything. Maybe you just need a few months of fun, or maybe you're looking for a completely new lifestyle. It doesn't matter if you're looking for a gap year or you're trying to start a whole new life abroad. You can and will figure out all the challenges ahead of you. Many others have walked before you and done that exact thing.

## The shoulders of giants

*'You can't just dabble in passion. It's all or nothing.'*

STEVEN K ROBERTS

Life, on paper, was good. But something was missing; it was something loud and unignorable, leaking in from all corners of life. Suburban life in Ohio just wasn't holding Steven K Roberts' attention.

'My reality had become one of performing decreasingly interesting tasks for the sole purpose of paying bills, supporting a lifestyle I didn't like in a house I didn't like in a city I didn't like,' Steven wrote.[1] Despite its perfectly adequate appearance, the routine was colourless and it led Steven to ask a question that would change his life and silently signal the start of a new movement: 'Could it still be possible to construct a lifestyle entirely of passions or was losing the spark a sadly inevitable part of growing up?'

Steven made a list of passions that covered all areas of life, from lifelong learning to adventure to romance and more. An unlikely pairing started to come into focus in the foreground: computer technology and long-distance cycling. Looking for a way to combine them, Steven became captivated by a realization: *if you can work from home, you can work from anywhere.*

He wanted to do what seemed implausible: take his career as a technology writer with him as he explored the US by bicycle. This initial idea was monolithic, but Steven began carving away at it. He and his team developed a custom eight-foot recumbent bicycle, which Steven named the *Winnebiko*, and fitted it out with a state-of-the-art computer system, antennas, solar panels, a complete camping setup and more – everything he needed to live and work from the road. One sunny day in September after six months of feverish preparation, he cycled off, leaving Ohioan suburbia and the indifference that it bred in his rearview mirror.

Steven was the first digital nomad and while you may be picturing him riding off into the unknown carrying an early-2000s laptop and a clunky mobile phone, his adventure began in 1983. He wrote his articles using a Radio Shack Model 100 portable computer, the first truly effective personal laptop on the market. The *Winnebiko*, fitted out to the nines by a crack team of tech enthusiasts who were close friends, now lives in the Computer History Museum. Steven didn't send articles through WiFi and email but rather through a payphone using an acoustic coupler. Compare that to our current tech conveniences and it's amazing that remote work today feels strenuous at all.

Don't get distracted by our current technology: digital nomads (or *TechNomads*, as Steven defined them at the time) aren't new. On a broader scale, we're just the latest iteration of wanderers, now equipped with the ability to fund our wandering long term and maintain relationships as if we live across town. The same invisible force that pulls you out of your office with your laptop in hand has been at work since the invention of the digital wheel. Yet somehow it's still too often viewed as a strange, even impossible, lifestyle. The interviews on the following pages tell the stories of digital nomads who worked remotely spanning every decade since Steven set off in 1983 and illustrate just how long the misplaced scepticism towards remote work has existed.

In the 1980s, Steven's *Winnebiko* was cutting-edge technology that most people had never seen before and it was a sight to behold. At a time when personal computers were only for hardcore technology enthusiasts, Steven and the *Winnebiko* were about as conspicuous as it gets and attracted public attention everywhere they went. Trade magazines, local newspapers, television news stations from around the world – the media attention was inexhaustible. As a part of daily life, the gawkers on the road were even more prevalent. The sight of Steven sitting on the ground in a T-shirt and gym shorts with his personal computer hooked up to a payphone attracted endless stares and enquiries. So much so that Steven printed and laminated an FAQ sheet and left it on the *Winnebiko*'s seat to inevitably be read while he was inside every shop and restaurant.

In response to the question 'Why computing across America?', Steven summarized how the computer system he built supported his work. He wrote, 'Because of the computer and electronic mail capability, I can travel full time while continuing to do business and keep in touch with the "folks back home".'

'*Home*,' he wrote underneath in parentheses, '*is everywhere*.'[2]

Steven printed off his FAQ sheet early in 1985 after already logging 8,500 miles on the road and explaining himself countless times. Most onlookers were fuelled by innocent curiosity, while some were so confused that they called the police. Steven smiled and laughed as he told me these stories and it makes me think that the public fascination didn't stem from the technology alone but from the enthusiasm that they saw on display. That enthusiasm was contagious.

And these days, it's practically all you need to create a *TechNomadic* lifestyle for yourself.

## What it takes to be a digital nomad

Anyone with an online income stream, WiFi connection and the ability to travel can become a digital nomad. But just because you can, doesn't mean you should. In fact, there's a specific genre of traveller that I hope *doesn't* read this book and flood the streets of whatever city is deemed the next must-visit digital nomad destination, and that's the excessive party traveller. Such travellers are more excited about visiting Pablo Escobar's grave and trying the local cocaine than Colombia's food, music, welcoming people or natural beauty. When asked what they liked about a certain destination, they'll reference the illegal locally grown hallucinogens and the nightly party scene, often dominated by foreigners and disliked by locals. In extreme cases, governments have even proactively unleashed campaigns discouraging these types of tourists from coming to their communities.

Travellers who enjoy alcohol are not a problem, but tourists whose behaviour negatively affects the local community are. Party tourists often leave a mess for locals, turning what should have been a lovely cultural experience into a disrespectful interaction. If I were to institute a digital nomad code, it would go something like this: 'When I go abroad as a digital nomad, I will always be a humble guest in someone else's home. I will have an open mind, not assuming that my culture, ideas or way of living are the only right way. And I will minimize my negative impact.'

We are guests, as digital nomads. And if the feeling of being a guest doesn't excite you, then I think you should carefully reconsider whether this lifestyle is right for you. That idea should thrill you. Trying new foods, walking around unfamiliar grocery shops and having to pronounce new words in new languages should put butterflies in your stomach. It's a gift. A big one and one that will lead you to grow in radical ways. Give it a chance and this lifestyle will make you a better person. Commit to having a decidedly open heart, curious mind and willingness to act and your life's trajectory is going to change.

I would never say that *everyone* should become a digital nomad. But everyone who's interested, who wants to travel in a considerate way, should. If you're looking for an answer to the question 'should I become a digital nomad?', then the answer is yes. Every detail can and will be figured out and I'd reckon that you've already navigated much more risky and difficult situations. Anyone who pursued a university degree took a bigger leap of faith. Anyone with children has jumped into waters much more unknown. This jump is not as treacherous as it looks.

*'No one regrets travelling'* is a comment that I'll never forget reading in a Facebook group years ago when I was calculating whether the risk of becoming a digital nomad was worth it. It's a sentence that changed my life forever. In ways, my trip in 2017 never ended. I moved to Bert-Jan's country, the Netherlands, in 2018, where I spent years building my online work further and becoming a citizen. My

online business, Writing From Nowhere, was technically started in a hostel in London, but in a much more honest sense the seed was planted in 2016 when my body started rejecting the corporate world like a bad organ transplant. After living in the Netherlands and exploring Europe for five years, Bert-Jan and I got rid of all our things and became full-time digital nomads again, with no idea of when or where we'll stop.

Every page of this book could be a litany of the blessings, opportunities and experiences that remote work has brought into my life. It's nothing short of a miracle and it never would have happened without the encouragement and advice I received online all those years ago. Now, I'm here to encourage you. I hope that you'll see the validity in your pursuit of new experiences, fun and fulfilment. If we ever have the joy of crossing paths in real life, and I hope that we do, promise that you'll say hello. I'm six feet tall with long brown hair, glasses and a big smile. Come and tell me your story of what this life has given you.

It can take you literally anywhere.

# 01

# Surprises of living the dream

It was 6 pm and I hadn't left my workstation for the day. Cheery people buzzed around me from nine to five, but with my head down and headphones in, I had interacted with very few of them. The memory of the day played more like a time-lapse than something that I had actually fully experienced because I didn't genuinely experience anything other than my laptop, breakfast and bitter instant coffee. And no, this wasn't at my desk job in Chicago. This was in Mexico during my first week of digital nomad life living in a diving hostel.

That evening after the dizzying heat of the day had subsided, a smiling group of backpackers walking by invited me to go on an evening snorkel. I passed. My only meal of the day had been rice, scrambled eggs and beans, my go-to breakfast, so I needed to find some real food. I scrounged up a cheap meal from my assortment of half-used groceries in the hostel kitchen while thinking about work and didn't give the invitation a second thought. A few hours later, the group came back from snorkelling beaming and probably a little high. 'You missed it!' one of them boomed, echoing through the hostel living room. 'Bioluminescent stuff was everywhere on our swim.'

'Darn!' I said, while quickly Googling it and scrolling through the image results. *Not darn*, I realized as the reality of what I missed was sinking in. *Something so much more powerful than darn.* Bioluminescent sea life lights up at night like fireflies in the ocean. Instead of swimming through dimly lit waters, you're swimming through the Milky Way. No matter how many times I went back to that snorkel spot in the following weeks, I never experienced it. It's been years and I'm still kicking myself.

To add insult to injury, I had even hauled snorkel gear with me to Mexico (yes, even including the bulky flippers), so that I would be ready for such adventures. I made room for this gear despite having only two carry-on-sized backpacks because my new life would be full of crisp afternoon swims, colourful coral reefs and coconuts. Weeks after the bioluminescent incident, disgusted by the flippers' bulk and embarrassed by the misplaced expectation that I'd be spending all my time having scrapbook-worthy exploits, I dumped them. 'Gratis?' I offered with a smile to employees at a hostel in El Salvador. *Finally I was able to have a successful conversation in Spanish*, I thought, trying to find a silver lining as digital nomadism was officially taken off its pristine pedestal.

## Expectations versus reality

The first illusion-shattering realization of my journey had hit: I was the exact same person I had been in Chicago. Yes, I had jumped into the unknown and overcame an enormous mountain of fear. On my résumé of personal attributes I could now list risk-taker and international traveller. But underneath all these newfound victories that I mentally pinned on like scouting badges was the same sap: someone who had virtually no hobbies and routinely worked extra hours because they had nothing else to do. 'Fastidious worker' was not turning out to be a personality trait that transitioned well from office to beach.

It shouldn't have been so surprising. Even in Chicago I struggled to add depth to my free time. On a whim I had joined a recreational cornhole league which turned out to be no more than a drinking group that threw some small bags at a wooden board between pitchers. While it took little effort to find drinking buddies, actual hobbies eluded me.

A brief stint with soap making ended with my luggage being inspected by the airport explosives team on a work trip to Phoenix. 'Do you want me to call your parents?' a much older colleague frantically offered as security publicly held up and swabbed the contents of my backpack one by one, from my laptop down to every single item of underwear. Soap making was out. The moulds were laid to rest in the 'attempted fun' area of my apartment, alongside a collection of dead herbs and a stack of books I'd started but never finished. It begged a deeper question: was my corporate life not fun or was I not fun? I had taken comfort in always blaming my environment, but if I failed to flourish while living my dream life, then that highlighted a much deeper shortcoming than my lack of vacation days.

Should you choose to become a digital nomad, your environment will change. Instead of a grey cubicle you'll work from a balcony overlooking the Mediterranean or a sunny rooftop terrace in the bustling heart of Marrakesh. Instead of waiting at the coffee machine next to complaining colleagues, your daily coffee run will be on dusty cobblestone streets into tiny, crooked cafes. Your microwave dinner will be replaced by following your nose to find the intoxicating aromas of a night market in Bangkok. Every one of these dreams is true and waiting for you once you clear customs. But that's not *all* that's waiting for you.

Should you choose to work full-time while travelling, you'll also wake up with emails in your inbox and to-dos begging to be ticked. At-home life and life on the road can at times feel shockingly similar, or if bad work habits take over, even worse: a more gruelling grind, a harder hustle and a more chaotic calendar. But this time on an island with slower internet. It's an important expectation to understand before you embark on your digital nomad lifestyle: your surroundings will change but you take *you* everywhere that you go. No matter how ultra-lightly you pack.

While you may be imagining an entirely new version of yourself cosplaying this future digital nomad reality, becoming a digital nomad won't change who you are. Not right away at least, though the daydream can convince you otherwise. The fantasy is a lot like booking a flight: you see a list of package upgrades and think *I'll take healthier decisions, less time watching Netflix and actually practising Duolingo every day for $59 each.*

Even though your recent decisions and life changes may feel cultured and refined, you won't instantly slingshot several steps up the ladder of enlightenment. If you currently like to unwind after work watching reality shows on Netflix, you won't crave documentaries when you touch down in Cape Town. You won't suddenly prefer literature over scrolling on social media. If you love to sleep in and veg out at the weekends, you won't suddenly be overwhelmed with the urge to take hikes and scenic bike rides instead.

## Try this exercise

What daydreams do you have of your 'digital nomad self'?
Articulate two of them and identify ways to spend five
minutes advancing each of those aspirations this week.

Do you imagine yourself watching less TV? Grab a book.
Being more active? Go on a walk after work today. Take it
from someone who went to the doctor complaining of internal organ distress only to be told that they'd developed hip
pain from lack of physical activity: your habits will not
change based on the distance between you and your home
address. It was an embarrassing kick in the teeth hearing a
doctor tell me that I had tendon pain in my hip from not
moving enough. 'Sitting is death to the body. And learn more
Dutch!' were her parting words as I walked out of her office.
I wanted to blame it on the Covid lockdown, recent work
demands or any other reason I could find. But travel has already put my excuses through an X-ray machine.

I knew the truth: if left to my own devices, I will do very
little other than work. That included hardly leaving the house
beyond the three-minute walk to the supermarket during the
pandemic. It's true that travel *will* change you, but not immediately in the ways that you want. Instead, I think travel
changes what you need and how you see yourself in the
world. And it does so with the same intense honesty and lack
of sugar-coating as a night-shift Dutch doctor.

Travelling while working online is a lighthouse. It draws
attention to any bad habits and shines a revealing ray of

light to expose any self-destructive quirks you may have that sabotage your success. At the same time, it shows you how to change your behaviour and helps you navigate the murky waters of remote work and make it safely to port. Make it six months as a digital nomad and you'll still be the same person that you are right now, but with more cognizance in life. It's an incredible gift. How you handle that gift is determined by how you react to this new understanding of yourself and how you prepare for it now.

### When the shine wears off

There will be a very formative day in your digital nomad journey. You'll wake up, check your phone, think about your day ahead, make your morning beverage and get into your work. Unknowingly, you're speeding directly toward a rock-solid wall: a realization that will make you question where you are, what you're doing and how you approach your new lifestyle.

That wall? 'I forgot I was here.'

It feels impossible to not notice the lack of grey cubicle walls that were replaced by colourful streets, rolling hills and historic neighbourhoods. The impact will knock the breath out of your lungs. It's a silent yet blaring realization that you didn't wake up with gratitude and awe at your circumstances; you simply went through the motions.

Despite its devastating arrival, this is actually something positive worth recognizing because it's an enormous milestone in any new experience or relationship: the end of the honeymoon phase. Just like a laptop that now has all your shortcuts set up and software downloaded, or a couch that has its first coffee spill and is no longer 'new', you'll settle into your lifestyle and stop taking stock of every emotion.

Some of the acclimatization is unavoidable. After all, you can't pause every day to appreciate every single palm tree and parakeet outside your window or you'd never get any of your work done. But you can and should build a muscle against overlooking the good things around you.

## Try this exercise

From your current vantage point, look around and take stock of three things around you that you once toiled for. Maybe a coffee maker that you couldn't wait to use or a planner that you were enthused to try.

Part of the sustained happiness of digital nomads lies within a conscious practice of gratitude. With the novelty worn off, your day-to-day experience becomes just like normal life lived somewhere else with different sources of happiness and some new sources of frustration. It's not a sign that it's time to quit, but you do have to fight it or the same indifference that you ran from in your cubicle will follow you everywhere you go. Should you travel long enough, you *will* leave the honeymoon phase. But you can actually bring some of the shininess back and that starts with how you approach life today.

## The surprising highs and lows

The average person probably wonders if the digital nomad lifestyle is as good as it looks online and the answer is a resounding no; it's so much better. The adrenaline, the feeling of freedom and control, the constant cycle of challenge and solution, the realization that you achieved a huge goal. It's difficult for me to put it into words. How do you describe seeing your dreams come true? Everything you've seen pictures of is there. It exists. You can go to it. Visas and finances permitting, it's not difficult.

But this narrative of mountaintops and victories needs balance, too. You rarely see the downsides publicized. The loneliness. The missed celebrations back home. The health problems that go undealt with because of the headache of finding a doctor. The uncertainty.

On a bad day as a digital nomad, you'd pay a lot of money to be right back at your desk with your grumpy colleague sitting next to you cursing at their computer. With the same old home waiting for you at the end of the day, knowing where you'd wake up and how the following day would likely unfold. The continuous cycle of making decisions, relocating and acclimatizing takes a toll. When your life becomes so dependent on internet speed and turning in assignments, it's easy to lose sight of the forest through the trees. Or rather, the sunrise behind the laptop screen.

Here are some surprises, both good and bad, that you should accept before embarking on your digital nomad journey.

### Experimentation

While it's easy to stick to the list of tourist highlights and digital nomad hotspots, it's a beautiful opportunity to experiment with your type of living. Remote work allows you to experiment with different lifestyles without consequences or risk. Always wanted to live on the beach? Go try it. Daydreamt of living in a remote cabin? Choose your country and book your Airbnb right now. Have you imagined grabbing a slice of pizza and an Aperol Spritz in Rome for dinner after a day of work? Plan it. You get to discover what you really value in a travel destination and a place to live, without the expense or risk of having to move there.

## Costs

The financial cost of this lifestyle fluctuates greatly based on factors such as the popularity of the destination and the time of year. This shock can go in either direction: you may be shocked at the cost of a month-long stay in your dream destination or pleasantly surprised and ready to book immediately. You may find yourself spending even less on monthly travel accommodation than you do on your current rent. Most digital nomads pay for their accommodation in place of a mortgage or rent, so daydreams that were previously off-limits are now more reasonable than you might expect. When I went from Chicago to Central America, my monthly expenses decreased drastically. When I went from South America to the Netherlands, costs went back up. You have the ability to change at any given moment and what a phenomenal gift that is.

## Time

You've heard the cliché 'time is money'. When you're travelling, time is something so much more valuable than money. Time is an experience. Memories. Feeling alive. Finish your work for your day and you'll walk out your door into the streets of Hôi An, Istanbul or La Paz. *All you have to do is finish your work.* You'll develop a heightened awareness of how you spend your time, though a total command will require experience and improved work stamina.

## Growth

The blitz of unfamiliar situations and daily challenges creates a growth environment like no other. Navigating through unfamiliar experiences stimulates an immense bout of personal development. You naturally evolve to become a more self-reliant and resourceful person as you learn to adapt to different environments, communicate across language barriers, and handle unexpected and unique circumstances. Being forced into a constant active role in decision-making is at the heart of the digital nomad experience and it's a pressure cooker of growth.

This type of growth is very reactive to the challenging landscape that international travel presents, but there's a secondary growth opportunity as well: you expand your horizons radically by experiencing new cultures. Stepping away from your familiar environment and routines gives you the space and time for self-reflection and introspection. Travelling disconnects you from the givens of daily life, offering you a chance to reassess your values, passions and goals. Meeting people from all over the world and exploring how other cultures live expands your worldview and allows you to acquire understanding and skills beyond what a traditional life can offer. Discover new interests or gain a clearer sense of your identity and purpose.

## Confidence

Something I cherish most about the digital nomad lifestyle is the confidence it's given me. Not the confidence to walk into a party in slow-motion and turn heads, but resolute confidence in how I'm spending my time. I'm making decisions that reflect how I want to live and what I want to experience and those choices represent my aspirations and goals instead of my fears and insecurities. I've done things that I never imagined I'd get to do. Looking at my life since 2017, there are countless things that I would have wholeheartedly argued I *couldn't* do.

*Squat in a parking garage overnight when there's a mishap with the train schedule?* I can't do that.

*Have a doctor's appointment alone at a hospital via Google Translate on my phone?* I can't do that.

Or, perhaps the most revolutionary:

*Learn how to actually manage my time and stop procrastinating?* I definitely can't do that.

This is a truth of travel: you will shock yourself with what you're able to do.

### *Organization*

Amongst all of the sexy factors that make up your digital nomad experience proudly stands nerdy, slightly annoying organization. The organization of your physical and digital belongings will have a massive impact on your experience. Learning to constantly stay on top of things is so vital to your stability that it pounds you into the most organized version of yourself. Successfully managing your inbox, workload and relationships will become second nature as your stability teeters on them flourishing. This extra time not spent apologizing for missed emails and scrambling to meet deadlines will free up an incredible amount of time for cooking more enjoyable meals, investing in your hobbies and spending time enjoying life that would have otherwise been wasted. This will make you a better worker and person in many respects.

Learning to be as organized as possible is so vital to your stability that I recommend you work on it before embarking on your digital nomad experience. We'll dive deep into this in Chapter 4: Caring for your career.

## Health

Odds are, the travel lifestyle is more active than your at-home lifestyle. Every day, you become a little bit stronger, a little more toned and, once you move past the initial drain, more energized. It's like watching your body slowly come into focus. And when you're not feeling right, it's apparent. Digestive discomfort, headaches and even minor health ailments really impact your digital nomad experience. Life abroad forces you to listen to your body on a deeper level. Much more than in normal life because finding health-care is an involved process. This demand of the digital nomad experience insists upon balance, self-care and maintaining your health.

## Stamina

It's completely normal to feel mentally and physically drained by the process of working remotely. Sitting behind a computer for 8 hours initially takes an incredible amount of energy and finishing your work may very well take longer than you expect during the transition period. There's an unexpected physical and mental demand that will knock you flat on your back if you're not braced for it.

Frequent breaks help combat this. Most remote workers struggle to take breaks and when a bad day hits, the gut response is to not pause until you've 'earned' a break. Effective breaks aren't used as a rewards system. They also aren't responses to physical demands, such as bathroom and food needs. They're not supposed to be, at least. They should be routine pit stops to refill the mental fuel before your meter sinks below empty and drifts off the road with your flashers on. Or even just before your focus and quality of work start to deteriorate.

Learning to meter yourself is a pressing need. The fatigue of sitting behind a computer for hours alone in a hotel room, Airbnb or hostel is an intense type of drain that takes time to adjust to. The same goes for one of a digital nomad's other big drains: continual decisions.

### Decisions

After a long workday in our Airbnb, Bert-Jan and I grabbed our shopping bags, rolled up our pant legs and started the 30-minute walk to the grocery store with our feet in the calm ocean waves. After eight hours of work I would usually not appreciate such a long journey to the grocery store, but it was impossible to resent our surroundings watching the sun sink towards the crystal-clear blue waters of the Mediterranean.

With salty calves and sandy flip-flops, we shook ourselves off and ventured into the grocery store, where we shuffled through aisle after aisle trying unsuccessfully to use Google Translate to convert the Greek labels into English. 'Is this butter? Or cheese? Do you think it could be lard?' Bert-Jan thought out loud. We never learned the answer. The amount of time and mental fuel you'll burn completing what are, at home, autopilot tasks, is shocking. We ate a lot of fresh veggies and beans that trip, sticking to foods that are easy to identify and making a mental note that Google Translate is not successful with all the languages in its language library.

You probably don't make that many conscious decisions in your day-to-day life. Normal life is upheld by invisible pre-determined pillars, like around what time you'll get up, where you'll eat breakfast and how you'll get to work. These are all questions that you once asked yourself, but you've now coded your response. You'll get to work between 7 and 8. Always eat breakfast at home, unless you're running late. Drive into work. Sit at your same desk.

Remove yourself from a routine and you're faced with dozens of questions before even sitting down at your computer. The biggest question a digital nomad asks themselves is what country will I work from? Then, what city? Which part of the city? And where will you stay? Let's say you chose a hotel. Will you try to work from your room or go to a cafe, McDonald's, library or co-working space? Say you choose a coffee shop but then a colleague asks for a quick video call. Where do you run to take it? Back to your hotel room? Find a quiet corner of the cafe? Every junction of your day creates an avalanche of questions that all take conscious consideration and evaluation.

This need for constant analysis is precisely what draws you out of the autopilot state that so easily comes with a routine, but it's also heedless to pretend that this isn't exhausting. And the higher the stakes, the more draining these questions become. Nothing consumes more energy than the questions and decisions around safety.

'Should I go home before it gets any later or is it OK to get one more round?' Bert-Jan asked himself one night in Colombia at an Irish pub. He was having a fun night with some travellers he'd just met and one more drink seemed harmless. After the beers ran empty, the group made plans to meet up the next day and said goodbye outside of the bar, going their separate ways back to their hostels. Upon reconvening the following afternoon, it was shared that every single person had been mugged on their way home.

When a man with a screwdriver demanded money from Bert-Jan, he turned his pockets inside out and handed over everything he had: a very small amount of money. It wasn't much and the altercation ended as quickly as it began. Little did the screwdriver-wielder know, Bert-Jan's real cash supply was hidden in a secret pocket sewn into his waistband by his mother. It was ultimately a non-violent incident, but should they have all left the bar sooner? Was it a mistake to go out in that neighbourhood? The feedback loop is loud, endless and critical.

Decision fatigue boils down to the absence of autopilot. In a new country, so few decisions can be made without thinking. This awakening can sometimes sound like waking up to birds singing outside your window or other times like a blaring alarm clock that you want to snooze.

### Average moments

A surprising percentage of travelling is unglamorous: chasing a stable enough WiFi connection at a McDonald's in Kuala Lumpur, Malaysia, waiting for hours at a bus terminal in Lima, Peru, bad weather in Kigali, Rwanda, rendering you confined to your hotel room for days. These are moments to read books, play cards, talk to strangers and order a third cup of coffee to leisurely fill the time. Moments like these are often elusive in normal life. Remember to rise to all of the smaller moments along your travels, not just the big shiny ones at the mountain tops. Someone who fails to rise to the occasion of dating travel will never fall in love with it, or have travel love them right back.

## Packing decisions

No matter how much research you do, within the first week, you will be sorely missing an extender or cord or wishing you'd brought a different bag altogether. This is not that different from travelling, but, like everything with the digital nomad experience, it's just more intense. Consider this to be your permission slip to forgive yourself and buy whatever you forgot at home along the way. Forgetting at least one important item is a rite of passage. If you lean in the other direction and overpack, that is easily resolved: simply give away or trade your odds and ends from your hostel bunk or make a kid's day by giving them some free stuff.

## Social perception

In defence of my decision to be completely self-employed so that I could travel freely, I told a very close friend that people were paying me $150 an hour to teach them Pinterest marketing. It wasn't meant to be scandalous; I expected this information to validate to them that I could be a real professional and that the structure of a salary and a four-walled office was just one path in life. Instead, they responded: '*I guess on the internet, you can sell BS to anyone.*'

While your plans are still being developed, there are two groups of people to consult: (1) those who will share your enthusiasm, and (2) those with experience that can help. If a person in your life doesn't fit into one of those categories, then it's worth waiting to tell them until you have answers to the expected questions. The odds of getting uninformed reactions and bad advice are too high. And bad advice is much more insidious than it appears on the surface. It's not like an uninteresting video on social media where you blink and scroll on within a millisecond without giving it another thought. When people in your life sit down to share their concerns with you about your plans, the social convention is to politely listen.

> Don't people get murdered in [any country]? Isn't that just an extended vacation? What's *so* bad about life here?

Or, as Steven K Roberts' mom articulately summarized her concerns about his decision to ride a high-tech recumbent bicycle around the country:

> 'What's the matter Steve, you're going to be a bum all your life?'
>
> 'Define "bum",' Steven replied.

This reaction is particularly funny given that Steven's bicycle later ended up in the Computer History Museum. Many magazines, industry journals and news outlets covered his bicycle journey in 1983 and instead of calling his parents and telling them about his plans, he simply cut out a magazine article about his trip and mailed it to them.

I recommend introducing the topic to your network with a light touch, especially if their opinions matter to you. When disapproving comments come from colleagues or unimportant people, then you can simply change the topic of conversation and leave their scepticism behind. When these questions come from important people in your life, then you need to have answers.

Don't broach the conversation until you're ready to stand firm in your plan, so that you don't get pummelled with questions and knocked over before you're ready to answer. Having a plan and being able to calmly answer questions will help the people in your life have confidence in you and your new lifestyle by extension. Feel free to reassure them that this is surprisingly normal and in fact your friend Kayla has been working online abroad since 2017.

No matter how much money you make or how many hours you log a week, some people in your life will never shake their perception that digital nomads live on vacation. It can't be validated by career success or making more money. Protect your aspirations from people who won't accept or understand them. If you don't want someone's opinion on what you're doing, then wait until your plans have already been made to tell them. As illustrator Mari Andrew said: *'The people worth impressing: your 5-year-old self and your 85-year-old self.'*[4]

Once you're on the road, do try to genuinely communicate how you spend your day-to-day with your community back home. Send pictures of your work views, FaceTime over dinner and connect on the human levels beyond the travel-centric moments. Your loved ones, no matter how supportive, may very well struggle to understand what your life looks like. You're about to become an enigma to most people in your life and that can have an unexpected sting to it.

The gorgeous pictures you'll share online are nice, but your sunrise hike over the cobblestone streets of Montenegro isn't a summary of your day to day. Make a point to share the mundane aspects that don't feel deserving of social media.

Consider making a group chat of your closest circle and send them normal life updates that go beyond the postcard moments: send pictures of your breakfast, complain about the weather and participate in sharable conversations.

## Job

Regardless of your employment type, a day will come when all of the uplifting feelings your job once gave you are gone. This surprise can really take your breath away because, in the beginning, your remote job is your beacon of opportunity. It is the vehicle that enables you to embark on your travel experience and you should cherish it as such. Until, one day, you can't summon that appreciation. The feeling of freedom that you have at the beginning of your experience will fade. Wrestling with these feelings about your first remote job is not an uncommon experience. Initially, you should take the best remote job that you can find, but make it a priority to think about what you really want from your income source.

'What I think you should do is explore,' advises digital nomad Zoe Ashbridge. 'Exploring options allows you to find a path into remote work and digital nomadism that you actually love. It's important to follow what you love, which in my experience, is also what comes easily.' Zoe and her boyfriend Stewart Law set off from their home in Shropshire, England to cycle around the world and Zoe stumbled into freelancing on the road in South East Asia. Now, she's a freelancing advocate.

'When you love what you do, the money will come to you; I know that sounds wishy-washy, but it's true. And the reason is pretty clear: if you do what you love you will put your heart and soul into it and when you do that, you're a pleasure to work with and you do great work for clients leading to trust, more work and more income.' Fighting to discover what you love doing for work is a worthwhile and often profitable pursuit.

## Travel burnout

Indulging in a mouthwatering mountain of fish tacos at a restaurant in Mexico, an older hostel-goer told me something so odd that it stopped me mid-bite. In response to my sharing that this was my first real trip abroad, this man told me that he was *jealous*. It didn't add up; he had travelled and lived all over the world. How could he be jealous of a brand-new traveller who hadn't even broken in her walking shoes yet? He said something that I've since heard echoed many times by many travellers: 'I'm jealous that you get to experience it all for the first time.' That initial adrenaline rush truly is something that can't be replicated and it goes hand in hand with the burnout that all long-term travellers ultimately experience.

I know: this sounds unbelievable when you would give anything to be anywhere else. Before travelling, I would have argued that even a urinary tract infection was an exciting adventure when it happened on foreign soil. After having a UTI on three continents, I can confidently say that you should hold onto that zeal as long as you can because experience suggests that it will inevitably fade. When the shine of travel wanes, you need to be able to look your lifestyle in the eyes and be certain that you enjoy the travel itself and not just the distraction it provides.

The digital nomad lifestyle is not the silver bullet out of bad habits or unhappiness and no one should see it as such. It's a way into different surroundings, more stimulation and achieving goals. A more saturated way of living, with intense highs and lows.

These high and low moments are sometimes triggered by the exact same experience: take a waterfall, for example. The first time you hike up to a waterfall in a foreign country is pure exhilaration. The cold spray on your face, eyes wide open, butterflies in your stomach, you'll think '*I can't believe I could've just missed this entire experience sitting at my desk back home. THIS is living.*' The second waterfall? The arc of elation doesn't go quite as high. You compare it to the first and even if this one is actually nicer, you don't feel quite as alive as you did before. On the third waterfall hike, your mind will drift to your inbox and to-do list waiting back at your desk. Being fully engulfed in the moment becomes more elusive. Moments like these become sensitive, leaving you with the bad aftertaste that travel has lost its magic.

Ultimately, you realize that the magic feeling that was such a constant in the early stages of life on the road has been reduced to magic moments. It becomes harder to bring back the butterflies of excitement in your stomach or the desire for new experiences. Months of new occurrences have desensitized you and left you feeling overstimulated. The craving for predictable moments encroaches and you'll start to wonder if you should go home. Maybe travel wasn't your solution, after all. This is called travel burnout and should you cross over the emotional threshold from vacationer to traveller, you'll likely experience it.

Burnout from travel can manifest as homesickness, physical sickness, prolonged stress, exhaustion, decision fatigue, lack of motivation, decreased joy, apathy and practically anything else. You have to be both proactive and reactive with travel fatigue: you'll never prevent it from happening 100 per cent of the time and it's also not a sign that you need to quit what you're doing altogether. When this hits, it's time to identify which aspects of the lifestyle are *giving* you energy and which are *taking* your energy. Your first encounter with travel fatigue may be extremely jarring and it's a sign that you've moved out of the honeymoon phase. It's there that you'll find what it really takes to enjoy travelling long term.

## What it takes

'It kind of seems like a scam.' 'It's a rare occasion that someone says this outright to me about the digital nomad lifestyle, but it's often said in other words. It's much more common to hear 'It sounds too good to be true!' with a sceptical raise of the eyebrows. It's not a scam. Frankly, too many people have been scammed the *other* way. Wholeheartedly sold on the belief that foreign countries are dangerous, expensive and unnavigable. That working online isn't a valid way to build a career and it's impossible to build real relationships. Not only is this lifestyle possible, but it's easier than you expect.

My apartment lease in Chicago was up on 31 July, which would launch me into nomadism mid-summer. As the days got longer and the sun got hotter, I was still terrified to leave my normal life behind, but travel was getting so close that I could smell it. I sat in a meeting room at my corporate job wearing business clothes that I couldn't wait to donate and daydreaming out the window over the Chicago River. The building sat at the intersection of State and Wacker, with a train stop just around the corner. I could hop right on the train's blue line and with only a quick 35-minute train ride I'd be at O'Hare Airport staring at a flight board with hundreds of flights coming and going all day. My credit card had a dangerously big limit. My passport was valid. A plane took off from O'Hare every few minutes and I could technically be on one of them.

This thought danced around my mind daily. The tangible boxes were checked, but was I *ready*? It was a question I asked myself constantly. I talked to every traveller I knew and asked them for their advice. 'Learn Spanish' was one colleague's recommendation. It was added to my to-do list. A friend told me 'ignore the first day; first days are always terrible.' Noted. First days don't count. A backpacker that I met in Phoenix a few months prior told me to volunteer with WorkAway to save money. 'Pick a hostel – lots of other travellers around and they have to follow a specific set of laws to stay open, unlike if you volunteer in someone's home.' Brilliant. Written down. I joined WorkAway and found a hostel placement in Cozumel.

It was the intangible side of the lifestyle that I was most concerned with. Beyond the technical hurdles, you should focus on the emotional side of sustaining a happy nomadic life as well. The emotional surprises are the ones that will make you question if you're on the right path more than anything else and as your friend who works online and travels, I want to set you up with realistic expectations.

There will be disappointments and bumps in the road; it's OK when they happen. That's just life and the bumps make good travel tales anyway. I don't think there's a single great travel story that doesn't include a wrong turn, a flat tyre or ripped trousers. If you were to grab a drink with a group of digital nomads tonight, you'd hear stories just like these, all sounding like episodes of Friends. *The one where a huge bottle of shampoo leaked and completely saturated my MacBook. The one where a monkey stole my phone. The one where the hostel flooded.*

Who carries that much shampoo at once?! We'd all laugh and get another round. These stories are the lingua franca between travellers.

There are no ups without the downs and isn't the flatlining day-to-day existence what you're trying to escape? As your friend who works online and travels, I insist that you have realistic, flexible expectations or you won't be at that bar laughing about your mishaps with us because you won't make it on the road long enough to have those experiences.

Are you still along for the ride?

Let's start packing your things and plotting your course.

# 02

# How to make your plan

In the Galapagos Islands and some oceanic regions lives a seabird called a frigatebird. Instead of hunting its own food, a frigate finds another bird that has already eaten and then shakes it until it regurgitates. Spared the act of hunting or foraging for its own dinner, the frigate then enjoys that pre-processed food as its own meal. I don't recommend literally applying this process to any area of your travel planning, but it serves as an important reminder that there are many, many ways to achieve the same results.

There are limitless ways to support yourself online, many types of travel and diverse approaches to budgeting and planning. Together we'll examine some of the forks in the road: employment versus self-employment, maintaining a home base versus going fully nomadic, popular travel destinations versus off the beaten path, as well as looking at a timeline and checklist for transitioning from normality to travel.

Rather than dictating which approach is better (those friendly debates are better had over a beer at a backpacker bar in Chiang Mai), I'll tell you what factors to weigh so that you can make a plan that suits your current needs. Remember the frigate as you research and make your plan: there are many ways to achieve the same result. Not only will this reminder help you keep an open mind to unique solutions and possibilities, it will also help explain the vast and some-times contrasting pieces of advice that you'll read as you research. You could spend every waking moment of the next three months consuming advice about the digital nomad lifestyle and much of it would contradict itself.

There are a lot of big questions to answer when making your plan: employment type, travel destinations and ways to pack up your normal life. As long as what you do is ethical, there are no right or wrong answers. I'll help you understand the options you have and find the path that feels most natural for you. As you explore all the different ways to hunt for your food, remember the frigate.

## Making money while travelling

It's a question Krystal Nagle gets all the time: 'When are you two going to quit your corporate jobs and go full time on your photography business?' The answer is always the same: *'We're not.'* Corporate life isn't something Krystal and her husband Eric feel the need to flee. 'We love the balance and the reliability with benefits,' Krystal shared about her corporate job working as a project manager. The photography business that she and Eric share creating content for Airbnb rentals is a passion, not an escape plan. It's the perfect marriage of interests: photography and travel. And with their full-time corporate roles being remote, they get to travel as much as they like.

The initial transition from *the* office to *home* office in 2020 wasn't without its learning curve. Krystal is naturally introverted and focused and she found her work speed accelerated in the home-office environment. Eric's an extrovert; he thrived in the busy buzz of the office and had to relearn how to be energized, but working from home together was a blast. Putting their newly regained commute time and lunch hours into the business was a no-brainer and Krystal and Eric had created two reliable streams of remote income. In 2021, they launched themselves as part-time digital nomads, leaving a home base behind in Pennsylvania. They drove all over the US, living out of Airbnbs, working full time for their corporate jobs and running their business on the side.

While it was a dream come true, it also came with surprises. Krystal and Eric had already gone through the initial recalibration that's required when you go remote, but they weren't entirely prepared for the second wave that hits when you leave your home office behind. The constant stimulation initially took its toll. There were days when sightseeing stopped being a fun reprieve and ended up being the very thing they needed a break from. It's the exact reason that Krystal doesn't want to exchange her corporate role for her photography business: 'I want this passion to stay a passion and not turn it into a need.'

Krystal and Eric still love travel. Beyond their road trips around the US, they've also taken shorter trips in Europe. And when other areas of life required more attention, they stayed put in their cosy suburban home, spending months caretaking for a family member recovering from surgery and tending to their own health needs. Their next big travel chapter comes in the form of a custom-built van that they're going to live in and travel from full time. They've built a sturdy and well-balanced foundation from which they work and play. And they did it on their own terms, which is exactly what the digital nomad lifestyle is all about.

If you already have a remote job or an online business, then you can flip ahead to the section on packing up normality. For those who are searching for an online job, you have to decide if you're going to take the bike or the bus.

### *The bus versus the bike*

Will you be taking the bus or riding your bike? This is a useful metaphor for exploring the different employment opportunities of the remote work world.

Let's start with the bus. Imagine yourself exhausted on your way home from work. You hop on the bus and have no energy left, but thankfully that doesn't affect how quickly you arrive at your destination. It doesn't matter how you show up – the bus travels at the same speed.

A bike, meanwhile, is controlled by your effort. You can pedal twice as quickly and arrive at your destination in half the time. The inverse can also happen: imagine taking your bike home when you're exhausted – your options are to sleep on the side of the road or pedal until you get there.

Many jobs are bus jobs. Let's look at the example of teaching music: a singer is hired by a music school to teach vocal lessons. The music school advertises the programme and interested students sign up to take lessons with the singer. On Monday, that teacher must teach five 30-minute voice lessons over Zoom. Their goal is pass/fail: pass by teaching the lessons, fail by not teaching the lessons.

Whether that teacher gives the best voice lesson of their life or does the bare minimum, they're going to be paid the same amount of money and that lesson will take the same amount of time. A 30-minute lesson will not go by more quickly with more enthusiasm and twice the amount of positive encouragement. Over time, of course, the teacher's performance will ultimately influence their success. Students will be less compelled to buy another block of lessons if they feel their teacher isn't as engaging and passionate as they expected. But in an individual lesson, in order to succeed, the teacher simply has to sustain their task for the intended amount of time. That is a bus task: the goal is to complete the lesson. Ideally, they would complete it well, but it's not a requirement to get paid. The bus is synonymous with the time-for-money working model.

Now let's look at the workload of the owner of that music school. They're pedalling on the bike. That same day, their goal is to sign up five new students for voice lessons. If they go to a park and meet five interested parents who are convinced to sign up their kids, they could complete their task within the same time frame as one 30-minute lesson. But success isn't guaranteed. They could spend their entire day and not accomplish their task. This task is like riding a bike and it's synonymous with the outcome-based work model. Both of these approaches to work have their pros and cons.

Consider these pros of taking the bus:

- **No overworking**. This provides a more manageable work–life balance, given that you know up front how many hours you'll have to work.
- **You're responsible for less**. The speed and direction are set by the driver. But this can also be negative.

Also consider these cons of taking the bus:

- **Lack of control**. It's impossible to go faster, no matter how much energy you invest.
- **Time-for-money exchange**. Working harder doesn't make you more money; more money comes only from giving more of your time.

Across from the bus, we have the bike. Consider these pros of taking a bike:

- **You can work smarter**. Complete your tasks in half the time and get hours of your day back to enjoy the fruits of your labour.

- **Your income is scalable**. After increasing your work speed, you can take on more projects and be compensated more.

There are also cons of taking the bike:

- **Uncertainty**. Maybe you'll arrive at noon and maybe you'll arrive at midnight.

- **Work–life balance issues**. 'Clocking out' is difficult and burnout is common.

The bike is often the preferred vehicle for digital nomads because there's a less direct relationship between time/effort and reward. If you're able to complete your work in four hours, then you needn't sit behind your laptop for eight. While this can sound like a shortcut in a negative sense, it's a valuable way to work, for both the employee and the employer. The people you work with, whether it be your manager or clients, will be happy to see you complete tasks more quickly. It's an opportunity to improve productivity, streamline your workload and reduce wasted time. But this isn't to say that the bike is better. It's simply higher risk and higher reward.

While results-based work (the bike) is often preferred by digital nomads, there's nothing wrong with choosing time-exchange work (the bus), especially when you're new to remote work. The bike creates a paradigm where you can always do 10 minutes more and that can be very erosive when you're trying to balance your career with enjoying travel.

Job opportunities won't come with the labels 'bus' or 'bike'. In fact, if you brought up this metaphor to a potential employer, they wouldn't know what you were talking about. But it's impossible to think about *where* you'll work without considering *how* you'll work. You don't need to make a decision about the bike or the bus today, but you should pick up this lens later as you examine individual jobs. The more pressing question is: will you pursue employment or self-employment?

## Employment versus self-employment as a digital nomad

Late one night while staying in a hostel in the Philippines, Gabe Marusca received an urgent email. It was after 11 pm and he was technically taking a week off from his business just to travel, but… opportunity was knocking. If he wanted to open that door, he couldn't wait until the morning.

Both WiFi and mobile phone service were too weak to send the email from the hostel and because of the late hour, nearby restaurants or cafes with WiFi were all closed. Panicked, Gabe sent a message to one of the hostel workers. This person graciously got on their scooter and went to the hostel to pick Gabe up. The two of them rode through the village and up a hill where there was a stronger phone signal. They stood, sweating in the hot night air, waited as the email slowly sent and then rode back to the hostel.

That's a demand that most managers wouldn't make of you. But should you choose to enter into the world of self-employment, some day a situation will create demands that chisel away at your work–life boundaries. Every entrepreneur I've ever met has a few stories in their back pocket about a series of mishaps or unexpected turns that made them seriously question their relationship with work.

There's a lot of debate over what employment situation works best for digital nomads. Ultimately, the travellers who are the happiest are the ones who have arrived at a situation that works *for* them, not against them. That gift can arrive in any form. As long as it's legal and ethical, all variations of online work are valid. If your goal is to work online and travel, then you succeed by finding work that supports you in doing that.

Every person who's employed wonders if they'd be happier with a more independent work arrangement. Every person who's self-employed sometimes longs for the days of standard employment. Nothing is permanent and there are dimensions to employment paradigms; you can move between both work arrangements as it suits you or simultaneously balance both like Krystal and Eric. You can examine the pros and cons of the different employment models, but they don't provide a complete picture of what each individual job or business model will be like.

And the confusing cherry on the top: most of the advantages and disadvantages go both ways. For example, someone could say that an advantage of being self-employed is the flexibility. But ask someone else and they might say that an advantage to employment is more structure. Researching can feel like sorting through a basket full of double-ended arrows, but here are some factors to consider as you explore the different work types.

### Stability

There are many pros to being employed as a digital nomad. For example, you have fewer administrative issues to worry about. You don't have to concern yourself with filing company taxes or making sure there's enough work to do. A job where you're contracted for a specific amount of work every week comes with a lot of stability. Short of being let go or fired, you can count on how much money you'll make in the next two, four or six months. You don't have to fear the feast-and-famine cycle that freelancers sometimes live in. And if your job requires you to travel, your employer will pay for it and you can mould your travel plans around your work commitments to save money on big expenses like flights.

## *Earning potential*

Employment also comes with some disadvantages. Generally, the earning potential is limited. Just as you want to pay as little as possible when searching for a flight, employers want to pay as little as possible when hiring employees. This is the reason that employees are often told not to discuss their earnings and job salaries often aren't posted with many job listings. Most employers pay workers as little as they can get away with.

Freelancers who work for companies will deal with this as well, but they're generally paid more and have more flexibility. Individuals who freelance have an incredible amount of autonomy over their income. This isn't completely lost on employees – any individual has the power to increase their salary when they negotiate the terms of the work agreement. For employed individuals, this opportunity presents itself at changes of employment and potentially in between, though it's not possible to simply go to work and ask for a pay rise because a project is really difficult.

A freelancer's rate, however, is up for negotiation with every project. Even when working for companies with standard freelancer rates, a freelancer accepts or rejects every new assignment and can speak up when a project exceeds the standard scope and warrants higher payment. Every project has a budget range and freelancers actively aim for the high end. Failing to negotiate a salary when accepting a job will pinhole your earning potential until you change employment, but freelancers can recover and raise their rates with every new project. Online business owners and freelancers can also pivot what they offer quickly, making them agile to pursue new opportunities.

Simultaneously, freelancers are streamlining their processes and learning how to work more efficiently. They have the potential to take on more projects and then use the output from those projects (experience, testimonials, portfolio) to leverage higher rates in their next job. Raving recommendations and an impressive portfolio take time to build, but another online currency that's (financially) free is building a network and audience online. Having an audience is a big leveraging point for many freelancers and it's something that anyone can work on.

Freelancers are often paid more because they're brought in as specialists. When a company hires a videographer to shoot some drone footage for their website, they don't just get the MP4 video file, they get the drone, the editing and the strategy session where the video shoot was planned out. If the company tasked an internal team member with that drone project, they'd have to pay for the equipment and invest time in learning, planning and shooting themselves. A freelancer is the whole package and they can offer their package to anyone, breaking geographical barriers to employment.

## *Benefits*

Companies don't owe contractors more than a pay cheque; there are no other forms of tangible compensation beyond payment. Not needing to pay for parental leave or retirement means that contractors are ultimately cheaper for companies. This is also an argument in favour of being employed: your employer doesn't simply pay you a salary, they provide tangible benefits. There are also intangible aspects of being a part of a team, such as community and teammates.

Freelancers do work for slightly more than just a pay cheque; payout also includes happy clients or customers, portfolio work and recommendations. But sometimes you have a client who's over-the-moon happy but still doesn't take the time to write a recommendation. Some aspects of your payoff can be non-existent or delayed months. As a freelance writer, I've waited up to 11 months to see some of my work get published.

## *Community*

Being part of a team means that you're surrounded by people who are all invested in the same thing. You can lean on each other, learn from each other and understand each other. That community is rarer in the freelance world, particularly for solopreneurs or people who run their businesses alone without a team or business partners.

This can also mean that you have to people-please and appease more people. Little tasks like replying to Slack messages and keeping up with team chatter likely won't be written in your job description but will be implied expectations. Company culture must be maintained, even if it means spending time on soft tasks that don't equate to role deliverables. Ultimately, employment may reinforce the time-for-money equation that can be limiting.

### Securing remote employment

There are two clearer paths to securing remote employment: finding a new remote job or turning an existing position remote. Let's start by zooming in on the remote work job search. In many ways, the job search for a remote role is the same as your standard job search. You can utilize online job search boards such as Indeed or find remote work-specific job boards like FlexJobs. You can get job listings delivered to your inbox, along with remote-world news, via the *Work From Mars* newsletter.

Your résumé should be adapted for the remote workforce, particularly highlighting self-learning, which employers really look for in remote and hybrid contexts. 'These are roles where you have to self-manage better and be able to identify where your own weaknesses and knowledge gaps are, and then proactively fill them on your own,' advised Emily Szopinski, professional development specialist and remote worker. 'Job seekers should be proactive in displaying these traits on their résumés and be prepared to speak about them in interviews.'

Before accepting a remote job, consider asking these questions:

- Are the hours flexible? Does it matter what hours I work and from what time zone?
- Is there a desired level of overlap between my hours and the rest of the team?

- How many meetings per week/month will I be required to attend in real time?

- Are there regular check-ins with remote team members? How is feedback given?

- Can I talk to someone else who's on the remote team about their experience?

- Will the company be using technology for remote work and monitoring software, such as mouse tracking or accessing your webcam to see if you're at your computer eight hours a day?

Even if your team is entirely in-office or working from home, it may be possible to negotiate your position to allow you to travel.

### Turning your current job remote

Your travel lifestyle might not require a shift in employment, but it will require an honest conversation. Speak to your manager about wanting to work from a different location. Be prepared to answer questions about working hours and meetings, and have several concessions prepared, such as a trial period, working domestically first before going abroad and time zone overlap. Time zone differences are often the biggest hurdle, so offer to overlap a few hours of your work-day with the company. For example, if your company is based in London and you want to work from Toronto, offer to start your workday at 7 am when it's noon in the UK, overlapping the majority of your workday with that of your team.

Grease the wheels for success by modelling exemplary work habits now, long before you ask. If you're already struggling to keep up with your inbox, meet deadlines and be an engaged part of the team, you're less likely to get a vote of confidence from your manager. Propose a trial run with a set end date, for example three months. This can give you enough time to prove to your team that the situation is workable or help you realize that you'd be better suited to a different remote role.

It's important to protect yourself and your employer during this transition. Protect yourself with contract updates. Once you're afforded free rein over where you work, before getting rid of your home, get it codified in your contract that you'll never be required to work back in the office. Too many workers have been burned by verbal remote work agreements that employers didn't uphold permanently, resulting in sudden demands to return to the office.

Protect your employer by never lying about where you're working from; this can boomerang back in the form of huge fees. People who do this are called 'stealth workers' and they've triggered taxes and fees that have flung back onto companies, suddenly costing them tens of thousands of dollars in fines. Anonymous stealth workers have detailed the great lengths that they're willing to go to in order to mask their transient nature, such as fake Zoom backgrounds, VPNs and flying all the way back home from another continent to pick up a company delivery. The hassle of getting company approval paired with the ease of pulling off a completely remote professional existence may create the illusion that clandestine digital nomading is a victimless crime, but working this way jeopardizes your job and can cost your employer money if you're caught. Finding a flexible job or taking the self-employment path is a more ethical choice for individuals who can't get approval from their company.

## *Odd jobs in person*

As a digital nomad, your work will be online, *but* there can be scenarios where you fill the gaps abroad with in-person jobs. These jobs can be very steady, salaried roles, often language-based, or they can be work exchanges. A common type of work exchange is house-sitting. In a house-sitting arrangement, homeowners who need their home and pets cared for while they're away will look for a house-sitter to live there and maintain everything in their absence. This type of role can be found in person or can be negotiated formally online through a work exchange portal such as WorkAway or TrustedHousesitters. In my first few years abroad, I leaned on work exchanges like Bartender for free accommodation and low-paying roles like childcare to help bridge gaps. These jobs shouldn't be relied on but can alleviate some financial demands by removing accommodation costs. We'll explore these options more in Chapter 5: Managing your finances abroad.

## *Opportunity*

The employment paradigm operates on a call-and-response model: employers put out a call for a new communications coordinator, user experience manager, etc. and interested candidates respond via an application. The shiny appeal of self-employment is that you can build an entire business around any task, even one that comes easily to you and you enjoy doing. During the pandemic, people paid for virtual golf lessons, virtual doctors' appointments and virtual babysitting. If you're willing to build a business that's remote, or even partially remote with the occasional on-location demands, the potential at your fingertips is huge.

Almost anything can be turned into a service-based business. Take Jen Glantz, also known as the Bridesmaid for Hire. Jen saw a need: some brides don't have enough friends available to serve as bridesmaids at their wedding, or a bridesmaid has an emergency and drops out at the last second. She built an entire business model filling in for strangers as their bridesmaid for hire. But a job like assuming a fake name and pretending to be a distant friend of the bride that no one's ever met doesn't come with an HR onboarding schedule. The learning process for your own business happens in real time and your idea, website or packages won't arrive fully evolved and polished to perfection.

Every single job has a learning curve, but in an office-based position, you get paid while you learn the ropes and receive guidance from teammates. The stakes are lower and the path is smoother. Self-employment is the Wild West with no HR and no one to answer your questions. Remote work specialist Hanna Larsson suggests taking these steps if you want to start exploring the self-employment model: 'Speak to people who are doing what you want to do and learn from them. Start writing daily on LinkedIn to build your personal brand and play the long game with building an audience.'

So, is it worth it to be self-employed as a digital nomad when so much of your life already lacks permanence? You'll have to make that determination yourself, but I'll share how I arrived at my answer. My personal deciding factor in the job versus business debate was the realization that the company I worked for would always vie to pay me as little as I would accept. The cracks in my once ironclad relationship with employment grew when I saw people online building brands of their own. Some people's work echoed and kept bringing in money for days, months or years, while the income generated by my work ended every day at 5 pm. That realization went off like a bomb in my mind and I knew that I wanted to at least try to be self-sufficient online. I've been self-sufficient through my freelance business Writing From Nowhere for years, but that doesn't mean that I won't ever be employed again some day down the road. I'm doing what best suits my current situation, which is the most enterprising decision a person can make.

## Digital nomad destinations

Choosing your first destination is perhaps the most exciting part of the planning process, but it comes with a friendly warning: resist the temptation to lean back on your normal travel priorities. A digital nomad trip has very different planning needs if it's going to effectively prioritize your mental health (and not just create unnecessary stress).

### Step 1: What do you want to experience?

Imagine that today when you've finished working and you close your laptop, you're somewhere different. What is it that you would like to experience? Although it's easy to get lost in the endless attractions or bucket list items a destination offers, you won't spend every day browsing a museum, going on a trek or having your third Coco Loco on a Caribbean beach before noon.

To help you narrow down a world of options, ask yourself the following questions to find the ideal environment for your working vacation:

- Foreign or familiar?
- Hot or cold climate?
- Secluded or bustling?

- City or nature?
- Beach or mountains?
- Off the beaten path or bucket-list highlight?

Even if destinations are popping into your mind like bidders at an auction, don't go down that rabbit hole of specific destinations yet. It's more important to consider key environmental factors when planning versus choosing a specific destination because it sets correct expectations.

### Step 2: When *will you go?*

Summer is the most popular time to travel and I recommend avoiding this time frame. The peak season of any destination guarantees peak crowds and peak prices. Many destinations are equally as nice right outside of the high-season window. Even going at the lowest point of off-seasons is still completely enjoyable in many locations. It all depends on what you want to experience at your home office away from home. Before you commit to a location based on season, research seasonal hazards (such as wildfires or hurricanes). If you're going in the off-season, identify what makes it less popular so you can tell whether or not it's a breaking factor. For example, rain is fine but seasonal flooding is a concern. I'll share questions to ask your host before booking in Chapter 3: Where and how will you work?

### Step 3: What destination *suits you?*

We've arrived: the sexiest step of planning your travels. In step one, you should have decided what you want to experience after your remote workday. The qualities that you identified at that step should have narrowed down your field of consideration.

This may sound obvious, but an important reminder for browsing destinations is to pick something you think will be worthwhile for you *personally*. Deciding to go somewhere highly recommended just because it's hyped up doesn't mean anything if you aren't specifically excited about what it has to offer. For example, someone seeking a shiny, bustling urban environment shouldn't head to Bali just because it's popular. Likewise, someone seeking a lush, tropical escape should probably skip Paris. If you're not sure what you're looking for in a destination, start with contrast. Going from London to New York City is probably not going to provide a stimulating, creative escape, but going from London to Barbados is a different story.

Research thoroughly before applying for a visa and specifically seek out digital nomad guides to understand whether remote work needs are met. Some regions are host to big hurdles that normal travel guides might not mention. For example, in parts of South Africa the electricity is shut off for hours of the day to conserve energy. This is called load shedding and would come as a huge shock if you hadn't discovered that in your research phase.

### Step 4: Visas

Digital nomads used to assume the role of tourists as they entered foreign countries. The intention of tourism was never a lie: remote workers didn't work locally and therefore didn't see themselves reflected in the work visas that countries offered. Stating that they were tourists upon entry seemed like the legal pathway. Most digital nomads were genuinely unaware if or when they fell into a different legal classification. Even before digital nomad visas existed, many countries were aware of foreigners entering on tourist visas and working remotely and no one seemed to mind. Digital nomads didn't take jobs away from the local workforce and it was in a country's economic best interest to allow these workers to keep making (and spending) their money as long as they liked. The prevalent attitude towards digital nomads, from countries and remote workers alike, used to be some version of 'don't ask, don't tell'.

The conversation has now changed and the shift is extremely important to understand. Some tourist visas do encompass remote work, but others don't. You must research this on a country-by-country basis before entering the country and the advice that you get needs to be current because regulations are evolving constantly. Countries are sprinting to catch their laws up with the wave of remote workers flooding their airports. It's a positive thing: countries are eager to attract digital nomads. This has led to the creation of dozens of digital nomad visas, which allow remote workers to legally work and travel, often coming with other benefits such as long stays, tax benefits, the ability to lease an apartment and more. Visas are often affordable, quickly processed and can be applied for online.

To abide by the rules, either remote work needs to be explicitly covered under the tourist visa umbrella or remote workers need to apply for a digital nomad visa to legally work online while in a country. These visas are tailor-made for remote workers and digital nomads who continue to live and work on tourist visas do so at their own risk. While consequences have historically been few and far between, it would be a mistake to assume that this will always be the status quo.

## Packing up normality

'I think the most painful thing to part with is this couch,' Bert-Jan said and I nodded while we surveyed our apartment as we prepared to get rid of everything and downsize to two backpacks each. Do you have a mental image of a couch that's worth pining over? Whatever you're picturing, that bar is too high. I'm certain. This couch, while beloved, had been in Bert-Jan's life for 10 years. And this was its third home. Entire mugs of coffee had been spilled directly onto its forgiving cushions. It was that perfect dark greyish-brown colour that held no grudges and masked all secrets.

We once spent three weeks house-sitting in a scenic village in the Netherlands and the house was nice. Too nice. Everything was expensive and breakable. On our first night there, I walked over to the kitchen table with a cup of tea. I sat the mug down on the wooden tabletop, then, within seconds, realized I should use a coaster. I picked up the cup and a ring had already appeared. Panicked, Bert-Jan wet a rag and scrubbed the area. It took no time at all to realize that this was a terrible plan, but the damage was done. We'd left a ring and then a faded blob on the table. The entire house-sit was spent walking on eggshells and trying not to damage anything else – unsuccessfully, but I'm done confessing to crimes. I was mortified and beyond apologetic to the homeowners when they returned.

That first night back in our own apartment, I knocked a full beer bottle off the flat, wide armrest of the couch. As it glugged into the cushions, before I could even react to pick it up, I exclaimed, 'I am SO happy to be home.' Even though it was an old, frumpy thing and definitely the ugliest couch in our entire apartment building (Dutch buildings have big windows, who can resist looking inside?), it was truly the hardest item to get rid of when we prepared to become full-time digital nomads. Because sitting on a couch that was *ours* was a detail that we were letting go of for an undetermined number of months or years.

Getting rid of our couch and most of our other belongings was the natural path for us to take, given that we didn't know if or when we'd return to living in the Netherlands. However, it's not your only option. Let's explore the four ways to handle your stuff as a digital nomad.

### Keep your home and belongings

This is the path that requires the least amount of change and work: simply keeping things the way they are and using your home between trips. Short of pawning off your house plants and forwarding your mail, there aren't many changes for you to make in order to execute this lifestyle choice. It's also the most expensive option: in addition to paying for accommodation while you travel, you'll continue to pay rent or your mortgage. This arrangement works for people who don't want to be full-time nomads but instead want to flex the freedom of the digital nomad lifestyle as a way to escape the grind at home.

### Sublet or get a tenant

If you're not interested in being nomadic long term or ultimately staying abroad for years, then subletting or getting a tenant is worth exploring. This removes the burden of cost while maintaining the stability that having a permanent address offers. There are some risks associated with this due to the responsibility you'll have for the tenant/subletter. You should think through what would happen if your subtenant left without notice. Would you come home immediately or would you be able to cover the costs while staying abroad? This should be worked out in a written contract. Having a subtenant will allow you to keep your home and belongings, assuming the temporary tenant uses your home the way it is, with your dishes, bed, etc. This is a great opportunity to explore the digital nomad lifestyle for a trial period.

## Downsize to a mobile form of living

Like the noble hermit crab, you can take your entire home and all your belongings with you by converting to a mobile form of living. Common forms include living out of a van, in an RV or on a boat. Robust and active nomadic communities have been built around them, but this type of nomadic lifestyle does come with limitations, largely where you can realistically see yourself taking your home. While it is possible to sail around the world or ship a campervan to different continents, you should explore whether you genuinely see yourself taking those steps and if your goal travel destinations are largely accessible in this form. Travellers with an extensive budget can worry less about distances, with the option to pay for long-term parking or marina space while they travel elsewhere.

## Downsize to just travel gear

Travellers who wish to reduce their physical possessions to the bare minimum will find themselves downsizing to just travel gear or leaving behind a small number of things in storage. Storage can be found with a paid service or potentially with friends and family. A beneficial goal is to reduce the number of material belongings to the minimal amount before putting things into storage. Over the months and years, paid storage adds up, while the belongings sitting inside age, break and decrease in value.

If you were to put all your belongings into a storage unit today and open it up in five years, you wouldn't find boxes of 100 per cent still-valuable items. Some items would have become obsolete or gone out of style, others would just no longer be of interest to you and some would have deteriorated. You would find that some electronics no longer worked, some items would have become rusty, some batteries would have leaked and ruined the items they sat inside. Not all items hold value in storage, so curate your storage-worthy collection discerningly.

This is the lowest-cost approach to the digital nomad lifestyle. It's the best fit for travellers who want to travel indefinitely or those who don't plan on returning to their home country/region when they're done travelling. If your travel plans are open-ended, then downsizing to just travel gear is a practical approach.

Deciding what to get rid of is the first side of the coin. On the other side is deciding what to take.

### What to take

According to philosopher Abraham Maslow, all humans have a set of needs and these must be fulfilled in a specific order.[5] The same is true of digital nomads. Our hierarchy of needs includes:

1 **Physical wellness:** general health, safety and emergencies.
2 **Security:** crime prevention and keeping your gear safe from environmental dangers.

**3 Work:** your laptop and digital assets that facilitate your telecommute.

**4 Comfort and ease:** access to your creature comforts.

Your personal packing list will require research and careful consideration. A few easily overlooked items are a vomit bag, luggage locks, rain covers for bags, digital backups of your computer, entertainment and basic cooking necessities.

# Checklist and timeline

Consider this time frame and checklist to help you prepare, plan and launch into your new lifestyle. You can condense these tasks if necessary, but I've spread this across six months.

## *Six months out*

### Deflate your lifestyle costs

Make intentional lifestyle changes that will reduce the amount of money that you spend on a monthly basis. A few basic steps in lifestyle deflation include reducing your number of monthly subscriptions, adhering to a strict grocery budget and quitting all non-essential shopping. This will help you put more money into savings and will also be an asset once you start travelling. We'll explore lifestyle deflation and all the other financial topics more in Chapter 5: Managing your finances abroad.

### Generate savings

No remote worker is ready to leave for travelling until they have enough savings in place to cover lost or stolen belongings, medical expenses, family or personal emergencies, unplanned travel expenses and sudden job loss or income reduction. Start saving right away and put as much aside as you can manage.

## Sharpen your digital skills

Upskilling is an important action item for everyone who works in the digital space and it's a habit to start building now. If you're employed, then staying on top of your field as it develops will help you be a more competitive job candidate. For those who are self-employed, upskilling helps you keep current clients happy and allows you to raise your prices as you improve. Make it a regular part of your weekly, monthly or quarterly routine.

## Build community

Join the community of remote workers who travel. Finding other people who live this way – or who are trying to – will give you ideas about what to do for work, where to go and organizations that can help you. Join a Facebook group or an organized digital nomad community like the Location Indie community.

## Actively improve your self-discipline

Start immediately improving your time management, productivity and follow-through muscles. Your ability to effectively manage your workload and communicate will have an enormous impact on your career, mental health and overall success. Find a YouTube channel, a book or a podcast if task follow-through is difficult for you.

## Take care of your body

This might not seem related to the digital nomad lifestyle, but health problems are a surefire way to halt travel plans. Start viewing your health (both physical and mental) as though it's as essential as your laptop. Travellers generally don't visit doctors unless something goes really wrong. Seek medical advice for more minor problems while you're still at home. We'll speak at length about taking care of your health in Chapter 6: When things go wrong.

## *Three months out*

## Research health insurance

Whether you're thinking about just winging it without travel insurance or you're still picking your health insurance plan, you shouldn't wait until the last minute to decide. While a health plan can be purchased abroad once you've already left home, it's best to complete this step in advance so you know how much money you'll have to budget per month. There are health insurance options that specialize in digital nomads.

## Determine financial requirements

There's no minimum digital nomad salary because every destination and lifestyle has wildly different financial requirements. You need to figure out how much money every day or month abroad will cost you and upscale your income appropriately.

## Renew documents

If your passport and driving licence are set to expire anywhere in the next year, get them renewed. Renewing documents when you don't have a permanent address can be problematic, so consider renewing them in any case.

### Go to the dentist

This isn't a sexy tip, but a cavity or toothache is one of the last things you want to have to deal with while abroad. If you have dental insurance at home, get your teeth checked before you go. Tell your dentist that you're about to go on a big trip and don't know when you'll be seeing a dentist again – they might perform screenings that they do less routinely to check for underlying issues.

### Apply for a travel credit card

In addition to savings, a credit card is valuable for emergencies. Research thoroughly (suggested criteria in Chapter 5) and apply well in advance before getting rid of your home, as you won't be able to receive a card easily abroad.

### Get your travel vaccinations

Vaccinations will vary depending on your location and country of origin, but get your paperwork and any necessary jabs in advance. Make copies of all your paperwork and store these with your other important travel documents: you'll be denied entry in some cases without proof of vaccinations.

### Get new glasses

If you depend on glasses to live your everyday life, consider getting a new pair before you go. What better way to see the world than with a fresh prescription? Plus, save your old pair and pack them as a backup. Opt for blue-light protection in the lenses – this will help reduce headaches and disruptions in sleep patterns caused by screen usage.

## Get your gear

Essential gear will include all the travel basics like baggage, travel items and potentially a new laptop (learn more in Chapter 6: When things go wrong). You could technically do this in a single day in one giant shopping trip, but if you plan this step, you can search for second-hand products. Getting gear second hand reduces your carbon footprint and will help you put more money into savings.

## *One month out*

## Forward your mail

Is a family member or friend willing to be your local mailing address? Iron out where your mail will go once you give up your apartment or house.

## Clean your laptop

See if a computer repair shop nearby offers laptop servicing. A good cleaning should include physical cleaning (for dust and dirt) and digital (for malware), as well as checking over for loose screws and water damage. Investing in cleaning your computer will help minimize tech problems on the road. For older laptops, also test the battery life and consider getting a fresh one if your battery is old. This can be a bit pricey but can double or triple your unplugged work time.

## Stock up on medicine

At a minimum, most travellers will want to stock up on their multivitamins and emergency meds, including tablets for allergic reactions, a minor pain reliever and anti-diarrhoea medicine. This step should include prescription drugs, which will require a custom plan based on your needs as well as the places you'll be visiting. If you have chronic allergies, take extra antihistamines – allergies easily flare when exposed to new food, pollen and conditions.

### Get extra passport photos

Some visas will require a passport photo when you enter a country. It's not essential to have these on hand before you go, but it's smart to have them in case you're caught off guard at a border crossing.

### Make scans of important documents

Make digital backups of any important documents that you could need for daily life or visas. These should include:

- passport
- driving licence
- credit cards
- marriage certificate
- birth certificate

### Emergency cash

Take enough cash to sustain you through three days of expenses (accommodation, food and transport). In some countries it's illegal to export their currency and you'll be forced to convert it or hand it over before crossing borders, but the slight potential financial loss is worth it for the security.

## Making your plan

I know how all of this looks: it looks like a lot. A lot of decisions, a lot of work, a lot more than you reckoned was underneath the tip of that dreamy floating iceberg. You may feel lost, but I know exactly where you are: you're standing in the exact spot at which most people turn back. Realizing that they aren't invested enough after all, or that it seems like too much work, many people will turn back and tell themselves that they wanted to become a digital nomad but it didn't work out.

It's OK to feel overwhelmed by the number of decisions ahead. Overwhelm is not a disqualifying factor; it's practically a requirement. I was overwhelmed too. It took countless pep talks from strangers on the internet to help get me through the hoops that the preparation process lays out. Now I'm here, looking you right in the eyes and whispering the same words to you that were once whispered to me: no one regrets travelling.

Shake the tree. See what falls out. You're being invited to believe in the Plan A version of your life. It's not the risk you think it is.

# 03

# Where and how will you work?

'You should've told me how bad the mould was!' said the horrified owner of a guesthouse in a remote Greek town. 'I did,' I said gently but firmly. 'At Christmas I told you that there was mould rapidly spreading over the entire bathroom ceiling.' Normally I wouldn't have held my stance, but we were both native English speakers and I had given a vivid description of the mould-pocalypse days ago. 'We'll need to spray it with bleach. And you should keep the windows open,' he said. It was almost New Year's Eve. 'We can treat it with bleach when you're gone so you don't smell it. When will you leave tomorrow?'

'We work full-time online, so we're here all day. Until about 3.30 pm when we walk along the beach to the grocery store,' I sighed. And we did smell the bleach, for days. This wasn't the first quirk of this apartment. Surprise number one came within the first hour of arriving. I sat on the couch and leaned over the armrest to grab something from the counter. With a gasp and a sudden flop, the couch's entire armrest and I slid onto the floor together. Apparently, underneath a couch-shaped piece of fabric were two mattresses and some armrest-shaped pillows. Then on day two, we found that both Bert-Jan and I were too tall to sit at one of the desks (the dual workstations being one of the main reasons we booked this Airbnb in the first place). Many of the walkable grocery stores around us were also closed, despite listing normal hours on Google Maps.

We couldn't have predicted this exact set of circumstances that would turn a beautiful month-long Airbnb stay into a house of cards, but the need to react and adapt is no surprise. All remote workers will encounter challenges to their comfort and work routine. Many of these challenges can be mitigated by proper planning and choice of accommodation.

Digital nomads don't have to work exclusively from their accommodation, but everyone will in some capacity while travelling, so the conversation about where you'll work has to start at home and expands to include both free and paid workspaces that you can access as a remote worker. Let's start by looking critically at the different accommodation opportunities and how they'll impact your work experience.

## What does home need to have?

Digital nomads are not homeless, we're homeful. Every place where you flip open your pack and pull out your toothbrush will become home for the next few hours, days or weeks. The process of packing up place A and moving to place B is both energizing and exhausting and the glass can feel simultaneously half full and half empty. A substantial percentage of that is determined by how well an accommodation suits your needs.

Arrival and departure routines will develop (I'll share mine in a minute), your accommodation standards will be refined and you'll stay in places that both disappoint and exceed your expectations. So what does this place need to offer? Look critically at these factors.

## 1 Sleep quality

This is largely determined by the surface you're sleeping on, the surrounding noise levels and the temperature. Some cultures sleep on hard surfaces instead of soft, which is something to be aware of as you're booking. Likewise, some budget accommodations will offer quirky bed alternatives like hammocks or cots. Experimenting is fun for a few nights, but lean towards a bed that looks similar to what you're used to at home when booking week-long stays.

A lightweight sleeping bag is a great insurance policy against cold accommodation, as well as frigid bus rides and nights spent sleeping in airports and terminals. Heat is more tricky to defend against. If you're sensitive to heat and you're travelling during peak summer season, look for accommodation that provides air conditioning and ask what hours the air conditioning runs – sometimes the air conditioning will only run at night and you're left sweating it out in thick humidity during the day. Extreme heat is not a deal breaker for everyone, but evaluate your needs.

Regarding noise levels, red flags include street-level accommodation, bars within earshot (check Google Maps) and comments on the noise level in the accommodation reviews. On Airbnb when you click on 'reviews', you'll see a search bar where you can specifically search for aspects you're worried about. Use this to help you weigh potential listings. Noisy accommodation can cause poor sleep at night and lack of focus during the day, which leads to your next consideration.

## *2 Work quality*

You can pay for an external workspace (we'll explore options), but since you're already paying for accommodation, finding somewhere that meets both your living and working needs will reduce your monthly costs significantly. Budget travellers will need to find accommodation that includes a workspace where they're comfortable enough to work 40 hours a week.

While a barstool, bed or fold-out chair can technically suffice, be honest with yourself: do your productivity and work speed decrease when you're working at a makeshift workstation? If your answer is no, then cheers to your resilience and mental fortitude. If the answer is yes, then you need to weigh the risk with the benefits. Your answer to that question will likely change over time. After years of working online, my productivity has increased radically, but along with that are more environmental sensitivities.

Also included under the work quality umbrella is internet speed. The 'digital' part of being a digital nomad largely relies on this, to a depressing degree. It takes a certain monk-like zen attitude (that I have not yet mastered) to not let slow internet affect how much you enjoy yourself.

There are two steps that you should take before booking accommodation to proactively avoid internet problems. Let's work in reverse: the second step is to ask a potential host (whether that's a hotel concierge, guest house owner, etc.) to check the internet speed and share that number with you. While it's important to ask for the internet speed up front before booking, there's no guarantee that it will be the same upon arrival. A number of conditions impact internet speed, from weather to building structure: large buildings will often have different routers for every floor of the building. While it's not absolute, it's still a non-negotiable step to take before booking. This is step two. Step one is to find your personal internet speed needs.

You need to arrive at two different numbers in order to understand your internet speed needs: your day-to-day (DTD) needs and your week-to-week (WTW) needs. DTD tasks are ones that you cannot go a single workday without doing. If you woke up tomorrow and your WiFi was too slow to complete your DTD tasks, you would immediately have to go in search of a faster connection. For example, my day-to-day tasks involve writing articles for clients, replying to emails and inputting data into Google Sheets.

WTW tasks are those that you don't do every day but you must complete on a weekly basis. Should you wake up on Monday and find that the WiFi is too slow for these tasks, you can do something else in the meantime and check back on Tuesday. These are tasks that are more flexible and can be shuffled around. My WTW tasks include creating graphics in Canva, uploading videos online and attending Zoom calls with clients.

When at all possible, you should reduce your number of high-bandwidth DTD tasks using techniques like:

- automation: setting up automatic payments, scheduling emails to go out automatically, etc.

- delegation: leaning on teammates or a virtual assistant

- batching: completing many high-bandwidth tasks at once.

To test your internet speed, search 'internet speed test' and select any of the providers. Run an internet speed test on your current connection. This will be measured in megabits per second (Mbps) and will give you two scores: download speed and upload speed. Create an internet speed spreadsheet where you track your internet speed results and specifically the slow-down it has on your work when the Mbps are too low.

This step can just be fumbled in real time when you have problems, but that approach will have consequences. I never paid particular attention to internet speed until one fateful night in a tiny but beautifully refurbished apartment in Grenada, Spain. It was late and I had a few vital files to send that couldn't be postponed. I procrastinated until close to midnight, only to discover with horror that the WiFi could barely complete these non-negotiable tasks. It was too late to find a cafe or restaurant with WiFi and the panic began to set in as files kept failing to upload. That was the day my WiFi speed spreadsheet and my internet red line were born.

Your red line is the speed at which you can no longer do your work. This will vary depending on the task; sending an email requires a lot less bandwidth than streaming a webinar. Next time your internet connection is slow at home or the office and it's causing your work speed to decrease, test the internet speed and detail in your spreadsheet:

- the impact the slow speed has
- what task you're doing
- upload and download speed.

For example: can't download Canva images or upload video files to Google Drive. Download speed 10.25 Mbps and upload speed 0.60 Mbps.

Next time you're trying to participate in a meeting and Zoom says 'connection unstable', test your internet speed. That indicates that you're getting near the red line for your Zoom calls. Knowing your red line and verifying that the WiFi supports your needs before paying prevents you wasting money on accommodation or workspace that can't support your actual work.

### 3 General living needs

The last thing to consider when deciding where to stay is access to general living needs. The most obvious factor is physical safety, but you need to be concerned with much more than just safety when booking accommodation. For instance, how will you get food? You need to have access to groceries (fresh markets or supermarkets), a place to cook (an actual kitchen is best or at minimum plates and bowls) or restaurants where you can afford to eat three meals a day. Finding these things within walking distance is highly valuable. Walkability is important for digital nomads, even those with a car, because you need to be able to close your laptop and immediately be immersed in nature, culture, social opportunities or entertainment.

Think about how much time you'll spend meeting your basic living needs when looking for somewhere to rent. While it may seem relaxing to take a long walk to buy groceries after work each day (and it can be, depending on the climate), there are limits to how practical this is when you're working full time. Consider being selective with your radius or those 'quick' grocery runs in the morning or between meetings will eat away at your day a surprising amount.

Bert-Jan and I have a 30-minute rule: we need to be able to access a substantial grocery store within a 30-minute walk from our accommodation. This doesn't include mini markets or night shops. Before you book accommodation, ask the host: what is the name of the closest big grocery store that will be open in [month of your arrival]?

Don't rely on Google Maps for this information, for two reasons. The first is that some shops close seasonally and this information isn't always communicated on Google Maps. Second, the definition of a grocery store on Google Maps varies from country to country. In some countries, entering 'grocery' on Google Maps will bring up alcohol shops that happen to also sell bags of salty snacks at the checkout.

In the short term, nothing beyond physical safety matters. Exhausted and overstimulated vacationers can pound some more caffeine to overcome a sweat-drenched four hours of sleep and assure one another 'we'll sleep when we're dead'. But what they're really saying is 'we'll sleep when we get back home'. As a digital nomad, you're already home.

## What exact form will home take?

### Hotels

Hotels live at the top of the price scale. They offer the ease of 24/7 reception and are often found in convenient locations, such as near to airports or train stations. Hotels are private and have to abide by specific laws to remain open, so they meet certain standards (sometimes hostels or Airbnbs live in the grey area in this regard). They often offer amenities such as laundry service which can make your life easier. Another plus, you can get a good idea of what the hotel is truly like through reviews online. This is theoretically true for any type of accommodation, but the more people pay for an accommodation, the more they scrutinize it and advise others to dodge a bad deal.

For digital nomads, the disadvantages of staying at a hotel include the premium cost of accommodation, the lack of a kitchen and (often) lack of workspace, plus the absence of community. Hotels are made for people who just need somewhere to sleep and they're not that nice to work or relax in. They're great for your first night arriving somewhere new or any time you arrive late at night and don't want the fuss of an Airbnb check-in.

## Hostels

Hostels provide many of the same benefits to digital nomads as hotels do, but with less privacy and more curveballs. One night, an eight-bed dorm room can be a quiet and polite oasis. The next, that very same room can be full of giddy, singing, drunk travellers. Despite the unpredictability, I think that hostels should be a requirement for all digital nomads, at least once, so that they can experience the socializing, fast friends and spontaneity that they offer. Hostels are one of the best watering holes for travellers and staying in one is the easiest way to make friends while travelling. While they may have a reputation for being full of single and eager-to-mingle 22 year olds, you can actually find a diverse selection of travellers in hostels.

Although some individuals above the age of 25 worry that they're too old for the hostel crowd, it often depends on the type of hostel you're staying at. To avoid party hubs, look for keywords in reviews online: fun, wild, excessive drinking and noise complaints. Many hostels have private rooms that attract older guests and couples. One of the best nights I had in Mexico in 2017 was spent reining in a hostel-goer's 60th birthday over margaritas; he and I are still in touch online. Hostels are beloved for their price point, but it's the chance encounters that make them really valuable to remote workers. Working online can be lonely and unstimulating and hostels represent the opposite of that.

Before booking a hostel, look to see if it has dedicated workspaces and a kitchen. Those are the two highest-value items to digital nomads beyond the social connections. Don't book more than a few days at a hostel up front in case the description or reviews didn't paint an accurate picture. It's not unheard of for some hostels to give away free drinks in exchange for five-star reviews, so it's prudent to get a first-hand recommendation or experience it for yourself before making long-term plans.

If you're nervous about staying in hostels, consider taking these steps:

- Choose a recommendation from a recent *Lonely Planet*. The hostel will be well vetted and as a result also more expensive, but it's still cheaper than a hotel and helps you get into the world of hostel life.

- Get a room that's just men or just women as opposed to a mixed dormitory.

- Or pay more for a private room to maintain your privacy while still getting access to the socializing, kitchen space, etc.

The hustle and bustle of hostels will be an asset to some remote workers and a liability to others. Start being observant about how you work: does background stimulation distract you or help you feel focused? Answering this question will help you find workspaces that are most conducive to productivity.

### Airbnbs

On the other end of the hustle-and-bustle spectrum are Airbnbs. While they're not Airbnbs by definition, also count guest houses in this category. Guest houses can be booked in person or found in local Facebook groups and they'll function the same way.

Airbnbs aren't prime for late-night arrivals because the check-in process can go wrong. Google Maps can send you to the wrong location or the host can fail to answer their phone, leaving you stranded for a night. This is what makes 24/7 reception at hotels such a convenience.

There are specific pros and cons for digital nomads living in Airbnbs, but the most overlooked differentiator is the isolation. While you can book a shared space through Airbnb, many listings are private and end up with you alone in an apartment for the entirety of your visit. If there's contactless check-in, you might not even meet your host.

The unique advantage of renting with Airbnb is that you can get whatever amenities you want: laundry, kitchen, pool, balcony. The quality range goes from a spare bedroom in the middle of nowhere to a yacht, as does the price range. The question to address is: does being alone all day help or hurt your workday?

## Free accommodation

The free accommodation options for travellers are actually quite varied. Truly free accommodation is rare, with the most mainstream platform being CouchSurfing, which operates under the umbrella of the 'gift economy'. Beyond gift accommodation, travellers can pay with more than just money: they can pay with manual labour or digital skills. These arrangements are called work exchanges, of which the most common is house-sitting. Through mediators like TrustedHousesitters, travellers can live in strangers' homes in exchange for their time and (almost always) pet sitting. The pets range from predictable household friends like cats and dogs to chickens, goats and beyond.

Besides the world of animal care, travellers can find homes and organizations all over the world that want help with running their businesses, farming, household maintenance and childcare. The most popular platform for finding these arrangements is WorkAway. For a specific focus on agriculture, turn to World Wide Opportunities on Organic Farms (WWOOF). You can even find work exchange opportunities based on sailing vessels through organizations such as Crewseekers.

These exchanges also venture into the digital space in the form of skilled work exchanges. Mikaela Donelan, a marketer I met in a hostel in Mexico, used her digital marketing skills to reduce her travel expenses as a digital nomad. Her longest exchange was three months with a hotel in Vietnam. 'I offered them my digital marketing skills to improve their website, Airbnb listings, Booking.com listings, pricing strategy, photography strategy and more. In exchange, they offered me a free place to stay and free lunch,' she told me. Arrangements like this can be negotiated directly with the hotels, Airbnbs, language schools or any other tourism-oriented organization.

## Where will you work?

I slowly opened my eyes and directly in front of me saw the upper arch of the sun touching the horizon. My heart began rushing and my mind hummed awake like a car starting, immediately ready for life. Out of all the countless hostels, Airbnbs, hammocks, tents and hotels I'd woken up in, this was the best view I'd opened my eyes to. As I watched the sun finish rising over the Mediterranean, I walked to the kitchen and started boiling water. Bert-Jan and I grabbed mismatched mugs from the cabinet and carefully walked with full mugs of coffee out of the apartment building and down to the seafront. Barefoot, we tiptoed with our coffee on a small pier, smiling and offering a *buenos dias* to the fishermen as we found a comfortable place to sit. This moment felt like a miracle, even though I'd been experiencing it for weeks in Spain.

We heard an English conversation slowly strengthen in volume and saw a group of retired Irish tourists moseying toward us along the water's edge. I don't remember who spoke to who first, but in a blink we were deep into the travellers' conversational dance: *where are you from, when did you get here, when will you go back home?*

'You're here for a *month*?!' one of the men practically shouted, visibly embarrassing his wife. The sun was warm on my cheeks and the ocean waves were quietly lapping at the shore and I couldn't help but smile, thinking about how these reactions never get old. The pleasantries lasted a few minutes and then they asked for directions to the main road and the six of us chatted as Bert-Jan and I walked them round to the spot they were looking for. 'We don't want to waste any more of your morning, you probably have to get back to work,' one of the women politely said as we parted ways. We did have to work, but it was the exact opposite of the work experience I once knew. Instead of a cubical view, behind my laptop stood ocean hues and palm trees. Next to me was a kitchen, where we made all our meals at our leisure. The WiFi was as fast as it comes. I was surrounded by a vibrant, comfortable, pro-ductive work environment. This workspace was a precisely chosen dream.

No matter where you work, whether it be your accommodation or an external workspace, certain factors will radically shape your work environment. Your choices range from crowded cafes (costing a cup of coffee) to curated co-working spaces with daily, weekly or monthly rates. Here are factors to consider before committing.

## *Workstation criteria*

If you're paying additional money for a dedicated space to help you work, then it needs to meet certain criteria. This is as true of a Starbucks as it is of a high-end co-working space. While some of these criteria apply more strictly to for-rent workstations and less so to cafes, these are still factors to consider before spending any time or money.

Your most basic working needs are WiFi and access to an outlet to charge your laptop. Next comes comfort, in multiple senses. Are you comfortable leaving your laptop out while you go to the bathroom? For a few hours or a few days, packing up everything for every bathroom break isn't necessarily a deal-breaker, but it does become one at a point. You should also feel physically comfortable working. Some working conditions, such as a bar stool and high-top table, may be fine at first but will ultimately feel clumsy for 40-hour work weeks.

You should also consider noise level. A busy and bustling workspace will help one person's focus and hurt another's. It's important to observe where you fall on that spectrum so that you can steer yourself towards your most productive environment. The cream of the crop workspaces will also have a quiet space for video calls. If you're looking to visit a workspace frequently, access to restaurants or a kitchen is also an important consideration. This touches on the level of convenience that a work location offers.

## Co-working spaces

Co-working spaces often have it all – the comfort, amenities and convenience to do your work well. They'll also have the price tag to match, with payment tiers covering everything from day passes to a monthly membership. Beyond the basics of fast WiFi and plentiful outlets, co-working spaces can provide community. The opportunities to network and make friends will vary based on the presence of a language barrier and whether or not the co-working space primarily caters to locals, tourists or both. When gauging social opportunities, ask if or how often the space offers social events and look for indications of socializing in reviews left by past workers. Not sure if a co-working station is for you? See if they'll offer a free trial day pass to see what the space is like.

## Cafes, restaurants and bars

If social media were to be believed, digital nomads do most of their work while sipping a cappuccino and snacking on a croissant at trendy cafes. In reality, you'd be hard-pressed to find a digital nomad who prefers the cafe work environment 40 hours a week. The wild-card elements of noise level, outlet access and WiFi speed make cafes unpredictable work environments. The cost is the issue that makes cafes, restaurants and bars a last resort for me personally when travelling. Beyond the expense of your food or beverage, there are sometimes hidden costs, such as an additional charge if you want to drink your beverage at a table versus standing up, tipping and bathroom costs.

Look around for clues as to whether working is accepted in an establishment. If you don't see anyone else sitting on their laptop, ask for permission before ordering and settling in. This practice isn't culturally accepted everywhere and how welcomed it is will vary from venue to venue. Become comfortable with asking for permission and always humbly accept a rejection. Bert-Jan and I were once scolded and shooed away from a table for simply playing cards while we were having a drink at a bus terminal in El Salvador. Having someone tell you no up front is a lot less embarrassing than someone telling you to leave.

### Free public spaces

Free public places that often have WiFi include public libraries, local universities, bookshops, shopping malls, hotel lobbies, bus or train stations and airports. Given the unpredictable nature of these spots, you'll need to evaluate the criteria every time, starting with 'is it safe to pull out my laptop here?'.

In some of these locations you can easily sit for hours without offending anyone or drawing attention to yourself. As we speak, I'm sitting on my laptop in the lobby of a hospital in the Netherlands; I popped in to dodge a downpour and decided to get a little work done while I wait. How appropriate it is to sit on your laptop in some areas, such as a hotel lobby or bookshop, will vary depending on the culture and the people working that day. A smile does a lot, a genuine request can go either way. Kind hotel employees have allowed Bert-Jan and I to work and even sleep in their lobby, while others have been completely put off by the request to sit for a few hours and irritably told us to pay for a room or get out.

While technically free, these spaces may come at other costs: noise level, comfort, WiFi speed, outlet access. The most frugal digital nomads will find themselves in these positions more often than those willing or able to pay for a cup of coffee while they work. Packing an extension cord and earplugs will help make these places more accessible.

## How will you work?

In the longstanding debate of 'where to work' there's truly no wrong answer as long as you get your work done. That's the beauty of the opportunity, but it begs the question: how will you work? And not the mechanics of it: plug in computer, connect to WiFi, start typing. How will you approach your daily task? With the structure of typical employment removed, you can do anything. As long as you finish your tasks on time, you can start every morning with hours of meditation or long hikes. Read an entire book cover to cover every day. Become a nudist. Adopt a nocturnal sleep schedule and do all your activity at night, naked. The magnitude of choice is both exhilarating and completely overwhelming.

When I first became a digital nomad, this translated to 'just work as much as you possibly can to be on the safe side'. I'm embarrassed to say that I lived in the headspace for years. I thought it made me more productive, but in reality it had the opposite effect. Without the guardrails of a nine-to-five present to you on the road, most people naturally lean towards either working too much or not working enough. It's natural for this balance to not come immediately, and it's worth focusing on as you find your footing in this new free-form post-office reality. That is, unless your company dictates your working hours, in which case you've arrived at your answer already.

If you're the one who will dictate and set your own work schedule, then it's time to start thinking about how you work best.

## The hidden need for productivity

There is an urgent, pressing need to understand how you can be a more productive worker, but this isn't to be mistaken for hustle culture. Digital nomadism is a pursuit of heightened intentionality and increased mindfulness about how you spend your time. On a micro level, productivity improvement helps ensure your job and income. On a macro level, you should be motivated to improve productivity so that you can close your laptop sooner and experience as much of your life as possible.

There will be many factors that influence your productivity, but let's start with a physical factor such as who you work with.

## Work alone or work with other people?

Does stimulation help or hurt your focus? Stimulation, ranging from background music to foot traffic to opportunities for small talk and general social interactions, will improve one person's focus and detract from another's. Your answer to this question will likely point in a decisive direction towards whether you'll be better served by a quiet, secluded workspace such as your accommodation or a busy co-working station.

If you had to choose your workstation tomorrow, would you opt to sit in a quiet room by yourself for hours? Or would you reach for a cafe or busy co-working space?

## Try this exercise

Imagine that tomorrow you're suddenly forced into a completely new work environment where you must work remotely for eight hours. Write down what your *least* preferred environment would be. What would be the last place you'd like to be on a busy day with high output demands? Then describe the work environment that you would be most *eager* to work in. Dissolve these different characteristics into specifics and you've started chipping away at an enormously important part of being productive as a digital nomad. The environment that best serves you will change based on your tasks for the day or how routine something has become, but this is an internal process to start observing about yourself now.

Working towards these questions from both ends of the spectrum will help make your preferences clearer. Most remote workers will feel this change as they gain experience and have heightened preferences or if a new job demands it, but it's good to start this process with intention and mindfulness.

### Task-based or hours-based workday?

When are you done working for the day? A healthy workday duration may present itself naturally, but it's often something that digital nomads need to actively cultivate to maintain work–life balance. Bus-based remote workers will have a more apparent end to their day and those with bike tasks will need to establish an endpoint to their workday on their own.

The approach that mimics normal life most closely is setting fixed work hours for yourself, for example working eight to four, and closing your laptop on time no matter where your tasks are at for the day. Or, define tasks that you wish to complete for the day and conclude your workday whenever they're complete, whether it be 10 am or 10 pm. Other options include putting work away when it's time for dinner (a flexible time stamp in the day) or when you can no longer resist the siren's call of going outside to explore.

Every approach to defining your workday has its assets and drawbacks. Putting hard timestamps on your day can feel unnecessarily confining when a week of bad weather ends and sunshine and blue skies tempt you to leave work behind for the day. Defining your work week may feel too abstract, so consider envisioning your ideal day instead.

## Balancing work and travel

Some remote workers will see all of this naturally evolve; others will attempt to create structure and then clumsily ricochet off the walls they've just built until they learn to find their equilibrium between travel and work.

Equilibrium is defined in the *Oxford English Dictionary* as 'a state in which opposing forces or influences are balanced'. Achieving it while travelling is so difficult because travel and work are indeed opposing forces. Thoughts of your email inbox will creep into your mind while you are gazing out of the train window at the Alps. Your mind will shuffle through your to-dos while you are walking around a museum. Intrusive thoughts about work will continually knock on the door of being in the moment until you learn to lock them out. Fail to balance these two halves of the lifestyle and you'll find yourself feeling guilty and distracted while both working and exploring. The pendulum will swing back and forth between the guilt on both ends of the spectrum until you're able to reach inwards and stop it from swinging altogether and find peace in how you spend your time.

It's difficult. And it's entirely normal to cycle through a rollercoaster of changing needs. You might start with a puritanical desire for routine and structure to help keep yourself organized, but then repetition will create a craving for variety. After making your workdays less repetitive and more stimulating, your days might feel overwhelming and unreliable, which will lead you to create more structure and routine. That structure will eventually lead you to desire some diversity in your days and thus the cycle will repeat itself. Personally, I run through this emotional cycle about every six weeks, but I survive it thanks to the structure I have in place.

## Travel structure

*'You do not rise to the level of your goals. You fall to the level of your systems.'*[6]   JAMES CLEAR

We were loaded up in the cab with all our bags neatly packed and were set to arrive at the Lima, Peru airport three hours ahead of our flight. Bert-Jan was flying back to Amsterdam and I was going back to Pittsburgh and as always I felt a bit tense about all the connecting flights ahead. I was leaning up against Bert-Jan's arm, emotionally preparing to say goodbye as we spent six weeks apart, when the cab came to an unexpected stop. I straightened up to look out over the dashboard and saw row after row of cars in gridlock traffic.

Bert-Jan asked the cab driver about the congestion and the driver replied, '*El Papa Francisco.*'

*Pope Francis??* I thought in shock. Like a computer program calculating probable risks, my mind naturally runs worst-case scenario simulations on travel days. The Pope visiting Lima and the highways being blocked off for his motorcade to pass through the city was not something I had mentally prepared for. A secondary shock set in that I was not nearly as aware of my surroundings as I thought I was. That was the first moment I realized just what kind of rabbit hole I lived in while abroad. This was a highly publicized news item that we had completely missed. As we sat in the gridlock, the scene unlocked a memory from two years prior. I was living in Seattle and the Chinese president visited. Residents were warned for weeks that the highways would be closed and we knew well to stay off the roads for the day.

A highway in a city of more than nine million people doesn't grind to a halt (or rev back up to life) very quickly, but after a long wait parked on the Lima highway, traffic eventually began moving again. Our cab driver started the engine and we slowly inched away. The wave of relief when we made it to the airport with time to spare was unforgettable. As was the secondary wave of relief when I realized that instead of having the cab meter running to determine the cost of this ride, we had negotiated the price in advance.

Being organized and well structured isn't a formality; it's a safety net that you will fall into. Structure can feel like a bad word, like the exact thing we're fleeing from. But the four grey, dimly lit office walls that drove you to run for the hills are not the same as travel structure. Travel structure translates to composure, enjoyment and reliability. The opposite of those things? Being unprepared, distracted and forgetful.

It's an ugly picture. I'm not convinced that you can enjoy a scenic bus ride when you forgot to send something important to your boss. Or that you can appreciate walking out the door with all your belongings on your back on a sunny day, surrounded by a language you don't understand and the smells of unfamiliar food on the air, when you've lost your laptop charger and don't know where you'll be able to buy a new one. Not to mention all the moments that you'll want to say yes to an outing with new friends, a hike or just a sunny afternoon but you'll have to stay inside because you're running behind on a deadline. To really enjoy yourself, you need good remote work hygiene. And I'm not talking about how clean your keyboard is (but be honest, should you be sanitizing it more?).

Remote work hygiene refers to the way that you conduct your work remotely. Being ahead of schedule, staying organized, naming your files correctly and keeping up with your inbox: these are all tasks that amount to the fundamentals of keeping your house in order while working online and travelling. This is the only promise that I'll make to you in this entire book: I can 100 per cent guarantee that poor remote work hygiene will detract from the enjoyment of your travels.

And normal work hygiene doesn't cut it for digital nomads due to the unpredictability of travel. You're allowed to have slip-ups, mistakes and unexpected curveballs when you're working in the office. Patience is a lot lower though once you're on the road. People will understand once. Maybe twice. But sending frantic emails from your phone saying 'my WiFi is too patchy', 'something came up with the train schedule' or 'my keyboard broke and I'm two days away from a repair shop' is going to erode your work relationships. Even mentioning your travel plans on a regular basis could create distance between you and your team.

Managers, team members and clients have limited patience for the troubles of travelling because most of them are at home or in the office. When it comes to productivity, normal employees are innocent until proven guilty, while travellers are perceived as being less productive until they prove otherwise. As Krystal Nagle put it, 'Not everyone always wants to hear that you're "on vacation".'

To protect your work relationships, income and mental health, always, without fail, be ahead of schedule on important work deadlines. Whether it's a vital email you need to send or a project that has to be submitted, the risk of waiting until the last minute is not worth it. Write that email ahead of time and schedule it to send automatically. Finish your project a day early. Condition yourself to see waiting to the last minute as being behind and develop the discipline to follow through on the intention to finish things early.

Growing up, my dad always told us 'on time is late and early is on time'. This is actually a quote from the author Eric Jerome Dickey,[7] and just in the way my dad commandeered this, I have my own version for you: *when travelling, the due date is late*. We'll dive much deeper into this in Chapter 4: Caring for your career, but this is too important not to touch on multiple times.

Balancing your work schedule as a digital nomad relies on the act of staying ahead of schedule and blocking off the right amount of time to travel. Small travel days and big travel days have different time-blocking needs. Big travel days are characterized by having multiple moving parts. After all, a flight is never just a flight, is it? A flight involves travelling to the airport, getting through security, one flight, or maybe two, waiting for your luggage, then getting from the new airport to your accommodation. While you may have done each of those things a hundred times before with no curveballs, so many speed bumps can and do occur daily.

A part of the need to be prepared when travelling comes from an enormous blind spot that you might not even be aware of: you're not in the know. If you're not reading the local news, then you don't know about any local events that can impact you. You might not be aware of local bank holidays, protests or worker strikes that can lead to public transit being shut down or other inconveniences. If you walk to the shop and see that it's closed for a holiday, you shrug your shoulders and set out to find an open restaurant or go hungry for a few hours. These surprises are a lot less cute when it involves bigger money: tickets purchased, not being able to reach a pre-paid accommodation or missing a day of work.

Protect yourself from these twists in the road. For big travel days, block off your calendar for:

- Day A: the day before you leave
- Day B: your travel day
- Day C: the first full day in your new destination.

These are days that you shouldn't be doing any work. If applicable, set up an automatic out-of-office email so that no one expects an immediate reply and block off your calendar so no one can schedule a meeting with you.

Spend Day A doing tasks like packing, doing laundry, visiting lingering local attractions, saying goodbye to friends you made, buying snacks for your travel day, spending your leftover local currency, plus downloading Google Maps for your upcoming destination and Google Translate for the language.

On Day B, I challenge you to be a truly unhinged traveller and not check your work messages or email. It becomes very hard to be in the moment when you're hopping on the train station WiFi and watching your inbox buffer and not update. People watch, read a book, play a game of cards, introduce yourself to other travellers, make space for your mind to wander. Become as economic with your attention as you are with your money and don't spend a single peso, rupiah or kuna on work on travel day. A balanced worker is a better worker, so treat these days like opportunities to improve your work–life balance and mindfulness. Upon arriving at your accommodation, log onto the WiFi and check the speed. It's better to know upfront if you're going to be able to complete your work tasks from home or not.

On Day C, explore the immediate area, evaluate the kitchen supplies and find the nearest food shop. Remote workers with the flexibility to take half-days may wish to do so for the first week in a new location so that they can get acquainted and have fun, but those who will be resuming an eight-hour workday should settle in quickly.

When it's all written out, it sounds a bit sterile and procedural, but adding structure to your travel is a high-impact way to improve your productivity, reduce mistakes and preserve your mental health and work–life balance. Taking off days A, B and C completely will set you up to be a better worker. This time buffer allows for train delays, cancelled flights and trouble getting into your new accommodation. It also gives you time to get settled in, explore and find a grocery shop when you arrive. Is it possible to work on days A through to C? Yes. But it's important to protect the joy you get from travelling. When holding a new currency in your hands for the first time or wandering through a supermarket full of unfamiliar foods feels like a chore to be rushed so that you can get back to work, you might as well go back to the office.

It's not necessary to balance your workload with these moments at home, but when you fly all the way to the other side of the world, it's an oversight to not dedicate specific time to them. These are the moments that you used to dream about and if you stop enjoying them, you're just biding your time before you lose the joy in travel altogether.

# 04
# Caring for your career

Travellers snored all around me as I was stuffing gear into my backpack at some odd hour of the night. I was catching a very early morning bus ride in Colombia and the regret that I had procrastinated on the packing until the last moment was tangible. In the pitch-black hostel dorm room, a dimly lit face appeared in a bunk next to me. I'd woken someone up and they had checked their phone to see the time. Hating to make a scene, I hastily finished stuffing things into my bag, swearing to myself that I'd always pack the night before from this day on, and hustled out of the room. As someone who always likes to triple-check an area before leaving, disappearing quietly into the night was not really my style, but I'd been travelling for months and my confidence level was high.

It shouldn't have been. Hours later when I unpacked my bag in Bogotá, something was missing from its usual place in my bag: my laptop charger. Left behind in the back of my hostel storage locker was my ability to make money. I didn't see an inconvenience or an unexpected expense: I saw a relationship with a new client being burned to the ground. The relationship with my only client, to be exact.

At that moment I was between freelance projects and was living mostly off my savings… savings which were now about to dwindle even more quickly. I sent an email from my phone letting my only treasured client know I was going

to miss the deadline and apologized profusely. 'I'll send it....'
When? I wouldn't be in Bogotá long enough to wait for a
delivery. The hunt for a replacement had to be done on foot
and it lasted for two days, during which Bert-Jan and I visited every single computer shop we could find. With every
stop my chest tightened and my stomach sank. Focusing on
keeping my composure, I absent-mindedly walked out of one
shop with my laptop still in my hands when a kind man
immediately approached me. He warned that I should hide
my computer for fear of being robbed, even making a punch-
ing gesture with his fist when he could see I didn't speak
much Spanish. I felt like I was making every beginner mistake in the book, for which the consequences were going to
be irreparable. Somehow when I had weighed up the risks of
this lifestyle, 'damaging career' wasn't picked up on the
radar.

Mysterious illnesses, sand storms, knifepoint robberies or
other unpredictable events aren't the biggest threats to your
career or travel plans. The landmines you should fear are
already with you: your habits. Procrastination, poor time
management and lack of self-awareness will put a much
stronger damper on your mojo and memories than any of the
more exotic concerns. As someone who's experienced both
parasites and procrastination, I can tell you that scabies went
away after two rounds of treatment but I shot myself in the
foot with poor time management for the better part of four
years.

The productivity stakes are high for digital nomads.
Higher than for other workers. Why? If your work takes one
hour longer than it needed to, then that time directly detracts
from the time you have to explore your destination. Even if
you waste two hours a week with poor work productivity,

that's 104 hours per year that you slid over from the 'exploring X country' box into the 'spent overworking' box. This extends far beyond your travels and bleeds into how you show up in your relationships, with your hobbies and how you'll ultimately lead your life.

Digital nomadism forces the conversation, but it's one you should welcome. This is an incredible opportunity to turn into the best version of yourself. The person who's focused, who follows through on their tasks, who can be motivated by the carrot instead of the stick. This is the moment to become the person you've wanted to be.

How many hours of your life can you get back by streamlining the tasks that you have to perform? How many times have you procrastinated or been unable to follow through on your intended actions and been stressed or damaged relationships as a result? Feeling like a victim of your habits erodes your confidence. It can also easily translate to incompetence in the working world. No matter when you're leaving, the task of improving the way in which you work begins today.

## Good remote work hygiene

Travel wasn't on Nic Bartlett's mind when he sought out remote work in 2007. He was happily working towards a postgraduate degree when his partner was offered an artist residency in France. Nic didn't know anyone who worked exclusively online, but as a brand and web designer he thought he could probably manage to make it work. The degree was put on pause and those six months in Cassis turned into years spent abroad in France, Poland, Switzerland and beyond. While digital nomadism had technically been around for decades by the early 2000s, there wasn't yet a mainstream path to follow and the technology left the heart wanting more. It was the era of internet cafes, Skype calls and clunky webcams. WiFi wasn't a given and the software took some patience. As a web designer, Nic shuffled around enormous files to clients in the US via FTP servers. If the connection was lost for a millisecond, the entire transfer was forfeited. A single transfer on a spotty connection could take hours, but Nic managed not only to meet the minimum requirements of his work but to thrive.

While always being honest about his situation, Nic didn't draw attention to his wayfaring ways for the first decade of his remote career. He maintained a US phone number and took calls using a Skype-to-landline connection because video calls were too much work for the average non-nomadic individual. So much has changed: not only has technology caught up but the social attitude towards remote work has done a U-turn. After the pandemic, many of Nic's colleagues in the US are also working from home. Company meeting convention is for everyone to join meetings via video, even if half the team is sitting around a conference table in the same room. Not only is remote work manageable, both sides are leveraging its advantages. Being eight hours ahead of his team, Nic gets to execute the majority of his workday in silence: no phone calls, Slack messages or emails. He may have to take meetings at 8 pm sometimes, but it's worth it to maintain his quiet workdays. His teammates even share in the profits of having a geographic difference. On deadline-intensive projects, Nic works for eight hours and then hands the project off like a baton to his US-based teammates as they're getting into the office.

'There are big benefits to being in the office, but there are also huge benefits to learning how to thrive in a digital nomad situation,' Nic said. 'You lose the ability to read a room when you're not in person, but you gain the ability to see through the artifice of "*are my shoes dirty, was this the right shirt*" and focus on what's most important.' Nic has been working with the same team in the US for more than a decade. After 14 years of remote work, his colleagues even travelled to Krakow to meet him in real life. Successful remote workers are great communicators, organized workers and empathic team members. Strong work relationships and reputations will thrive anywhere, even across oceans, if you invest in them.

In a physical office space, your reputation comes from much more than just your work output. How people come to think of you is a collection of impressions that derive from how you speak, how sociable you are, the quality of your communication, your confidence, how other people speak about you and much more. Many of those touchpoints are lost on remote workers. To counterbalance this, remote workers must conduct themselves professionally in a pristine manner.

Missed emails, lost files and unmet promises create as sloppy a gestalt as showing up to the office in sweaty, stained gym clothes. The wellness of your career and your professional reputation will ultimately rest on the quality, consistency and predictability of your work. Here are guidelines for creating good remote work habits that leave a positive impression on everyone you work with.

### *The 10 golden rules of remote work habits*

### 1 Stay ahead of schedule

If you always plan to submit your work on the day it's due, then it's only a matter of time before you miss a deadline. Condition yourself to see the due date as being late and submitting work ahead of schedule as the norm. Your teammates will love you for it.

### 2 Back up your computer daily

Every computer breaks eventually, whether it be from normal wear and tear or travel-induced injuries. A cloud-based computer backup system, such as Google Drive, will provide the most consistency; however, Google Drive requires an internet connection to back up your computer. Travellers who go through extended periods of time away from an internet connection should consider a physical computer backup, such as an external hard drive.

### 3 Name and file everything correctly, every single time

A file with the wrong name can't be found when it's needed, can't be put in the correct place and can't be confidently deleted. A computer full of unnamed files is one that becomes unnavigable and ultimately slow. This consistency is as important for you as it is for your teammates or clients. File names like 'IMG_9435.png' will inevitably waste your time down the road and look sloppy. Develop a file-naming convention for your professional files and personal files alike and use it every single time.

## 4 Declutter your digital belongings routinely

While you might not physically feel the weight of thousands of unnecessary computer files or hundreds of duplicate photos on your phone, there's a mental cost of surplus. Digital excess sabotages your concentration and makes your devices run more slowly. Having unnecessary digital effects will result in you spending more time on your phone or computer looking for the files, photos or emails that you actually need. Remove redundant files, turn off unwanted notifications, unsubscribe from unnecessary emails, delete unused apps and pursue every opportunity to be more mindful of your digital baggage.

## 5 Develop routines and consistently adhere to them

An effective remote worker knows how to manage their weak points and builds routines that keep them in check. This applies to everything, from how you handle your email inbox to how you pack your bag. Someone who struggles to keep up with their email inbox should designate one day of the week to catch up on every single email. Someone who loses things easily should designate a spot for every important item and run through a checklist before leaving. A traveller who knows exactly where their passport and computer charger go in their bag is a traveller who's a lot less likely to leave them behind, and someone who designates Tuesday as their email day is far less likely to miss an essential message or damage a relationship. Create the structure you need to succeed.

## 6 Be proactive instead of reactive

Working from a point of reactivity will create more stress and less predictability in your workdays rather than leaving you at the helm of how you spend your time. Instead, look for opportunities in every aspect of your work and life to be proactive. In your work, this can look like sending weekly check-ins with your team, completing tasks early, asking questions, prioritizing your workload accurately, being engaged in meetings and on Slack channels and seeking out feedback. In your personal life, this can look like setting reminders for recurring life admin tasks, automating recurring payments, setting reminders for easily forgotten tasks and scheduling regular catch-ups with family and friends. Disrupt patterns of dysfunction that you see in yourself.

## 7 Don't postpone small tasks

A lingering task, no matter the size, occupies a large amount of mental real estate. Kicking small to-dos down the road creates a cycle of avoidance and stress and impacts your professionalism. Designate 25 minutes each week to close out all lingering items on your plate. Anything that can be done in less than 10 minutes should be done immediately whenever it comes to mind. This will turn you into a proactive stress-eliminating machine.

## 8 Overcommunicate

Without touchpoints like talking at the coffee machine or chatting before a meeting starts, there's drastically less contact with remote teammates. It takes extra effort to maintain a personal connection with colleagues. Do this routinely on projects and around professional topics and also weave it into your personal relationships. Emails wishing a teammate good luck on a specific day, wishing someone a happy birthday or just saying hi can all be written in advance and scheduled to send at the appropriate time. Go out of your way to tell your teammates that you appreciate them and that they've done a good job. Send past clients messages to let them know that something reminded you of them. Reply to emails just to say, 'This is perfect, thank you, [name]!' Your ability to have exemplary communication will alter the course of your career and these muscles will atrophy if you don't use them. Go out of your way to over-communicate with your team.

## 9 Be intentional about how you spend your time

Being online all day is a double-edged sword and it takes most remote workers a lot of time to learn how to wield it. Fight distracted working, multitasking and half-working (for example, putzing around on a work task with Netflix on in the background). Your brain can and should be conditioned to know when you're in work mode. Keep those signals clear and have an easier time switching into work mode and then switching into relaxation mode when you've finished working. Don't cross those signals or you'll find yourself thinking about your emails while you're on the beach and thinking about the beach when you're in your inbox.

## 10 Reflect on your outcomes and be honest about how you arrived there

The most successful remote workers are those who hold themselves accountable. Accountability is something to lean into, not shy away from. If you didn't achieve the goals you set for yourself, be honest about why. Look for what went wrong so that you can get it right the next day. This is just as important for the negative things as it is for the positive ones. Remember the 80/20 rule? You'll become more effective when you understand what 20 per cent achieves the 80 per cent of your workload and success.

## The obstacles to productivity

Other people's productivity issues never really made sense to Nadalie Bardo. Her inbox, responsibilities and schedule were all well managed. Her work was organized, with systems that she had perfected over the course of years, and she worked from a home office that suited her every career need. It was a fortress of efficiency. But after a few years of non-stop career building and little else, some contrast was desperately needed. A digital nomad tour sounded like the perfect solution: join a group of remote workers who would live and work together while travelling to different countries. After much consideration, Nadalie pulled the trigger, uncertain but excited to see if this could provide some stimulation and fun that she had sorely missed.

The day before her flight, she sat on her office floor packing her suitcase. The once-perfect and orderly office was now disrupted by swimsuits, hats and charging cables askew in every direction. She didn't know it at the time, but this was very prophetic of what was to come: Nadalie's previously concrete productivity was about to be turned upside down. It wasn't immediate – the first few weeks she kept up her normal pace. But then a lack of interest in work crept in and she couldn't justify staring at her computer all day while in such dopamine-inducing surroundings.

Her travels were a joy, but she didn't feel like herself when she sat down at her laptop. She used to enjoy work so much and now she struggled to be alone with it. Looking around at the other remote workers, she saw that she wasn't alone. Many of her peers also struggled to perform their work duties at their normal level; some were fired and a few got so swept downstream in the FOMO that they quit their jobs on the spot.

Boarding a flight home months later, Nadalie felt like a changed person. This was mostly for the better, as travel had brought her so many cherished friendships and experiences, but she still worried that she'd lost the worker-bee version of herself that had previously existed. As she dusted off her home office, she got right back up to pace with her work-load. Productivity returned and she began crafting her next digital nomad stint but with a much deeper understanding of how she responded to working in a constantly changing environment.

Travel reminds you what you're working for. Ultimately, I think being a digital nomad will make you a better worker and a better person. A person who's more economical with their time, more efficient with their work, more grateful for what they have and more alive on a regular basis. But it's not a direct flight getting there. I haven't met a digital nomad who didn't have to evolve to arrive in that state. However, this doesn't mean you can't improve your productivity from home: you can and should work at finding the tools that turn empty platitudes like 'be focused' into actionable steps that you can consistently implement. This process takes time. Let's look at the three biggest thieves of productivity as a digital nomad: lack of clarity, procrastination and distracted working.

### Lack of clarity: impossible to-do list

Improved follow-through relies on closing the gap between intention and action and that happens by understanding exactly what needs to be done and how long it takes. Take a look at your to-do list right now: is each to-do item something that you can successfully execute today? If your planner is full of monstrous tasks that can't physically be checked off this week, then success is impossible, no matter how productive you are. Steven K Roberts, the first digital nomad, nicknamed this phenomenon 'the Roberts law of fractal to-do list complexity: each item on a list is merely the title of another list'.[8]

Conquering your procrastination starts with breaking down your tasks into smaller, genuinely achievable steps and prioritizing their execution. Maintain a continual feedback loop with yourself:

- Is this task a single task or can it be broken down further?
- In what order should these tasks be executed?
- When does each task need to be completed?

In the event that you fail to complete what needs to be done, ask another set of clarifying questions:

- Why did I not achieve what I wanted to achieve?
- What helped and what hurt my progress towards my goals?
- Can I see any self-sabotaging patterns impacting my performance?

A large part of successfully conquering your procrastination relies on continually evaluating your thoughts and habits until you learn where your problem areas lie. Once you've created achievable tasks and prioritized their importance, it's time to execute them without procrastinating.

## *Procrastination*

You might not feel that your procrastination is a real problem. And you could be right. Here's a test: if you decide to spend tomorrow doing task X, do you follow through? There's no shame or embarrassment here, partly because shame is not a powerful enough motivator to actually change your habits, but also because I'm in the club. I know the secret handshake and we can fill an entire night at the bar with cringe-worthy stories full of self-destructive behaviour. Procrastination can feel like a very personal failing, but it's your techniques that are failing you. The *Oxford English Dictionary* defines procrastination as 'the act of delaying something that you should do, usually because you do not want to do it'. Conquering procrastination is the simple art of following through. Let's look at where procrastination starts.

'Procrastination is actually driven by a lack of clarity for what logically needs to be done and overpowering cognitive distortions and emotions surrounding the task,' said college counsellor Kelly Carbone. She offered these steps to combat procrastination:

1 Objectively define the task at hand and why it needs to be done.

2 Identify all the negative thoughts and feelings.

3 Use cognitive behavioural therapy (CBT) techniques to challenge the negative thoughts in your mind.

4 Identify the smallest task necessary for making progress, apply the Pomodoro® Technique and complete the task.

The Pomodoro® Technique is a segmented approach to your workday where you work for a set period of time and then break for a set period of time. A common configuration is a 25-minute work session with a 5-minute break and a 15-minute break every 4 work sessions. There are countless ways to leverage this technique in your daily work, but my favourite is the Pomodoro® Assistant Google Chrome extension. Not only will breaking your work into timed chunks improve your productivity, it will also help you develop a realistic understanding of how much time individual tasks actually take. Once you've put procrastination in its place, it's time to execute your work with the highest level of efficiency and focus possible.

## Distracted working

A digital nomad who's set an achievable to-do list and is prepared to follow through on their work plan looks like they're set up to work efficiently, but something enormous could still sabotage their success: distracted working.

The negative impact of distracted working is easy to see: no one wants to spend three hours completing a task that could've taken only one hour. Distracted working fragments your attention and focus and results in a drastically slowed pace of work. It's something that everyone wants to minimize, but you may be unaware of how often you encounter this or what's causing it. Today, start trying to identify what fragments your attention.

These are some common remote work distractions:

- notifications
- frequent meetings

- cluttered or unkempt workspace
- phone or computer temptations.

If you're in a hostel, cafe or co-working space, some other distractions might include:

- passers-by and social interactions
- background noise
- lack of privacy
- visual stimulation
- slow internet connection
- shared resources, such as outlets and desk space.

Once you identify the work factors that fragment your attention the most, you can leverage productivity tools to mitigate these distractions. Refine this process and you'll experience improved work speed and more mental clarity.

## Work–life balance and mental health

'I know you're travelling, but I hope that you value quickly resolving this as much as I do.' That testy client email pinged my inbox while I was sitting on the bed in a hotel room in Rome. I'd just done laundry in the bathroom and my jeans and a few shirts were steadily dripping as they hung over the shower curtain rod. The smell of damp clothes was in the air as I read the irritated message and Bert-Jan was stretched out next to me playing a computer game. By all accounts it was an unremarkable moment. But something miraculous was happening: I read the email out loud to Bert-Jan with an eye roll, then quickly shot back a friendly message letting this client know that I had finished that task a week ago and they must not have read my previous email. I closed my computer, put on some Netflix and didn't give this email another thought.

The next day I walked around the Colosseum, sat on slabs of ruins that had been turned into makeshift benches and drank tiny cups of coffee without thinking about this client or the situation. There was no over-analysing, no wondering *was I not clear enough in my communication?* or *why did this client assume I had dropped the ball?* Just like Rome itself, that blissful nonchalance wasn't achieved in a day. It took years, and truthfully, I didn't even believe that this paradise of actual work–life balance existed.

Travel fatigue. Normal work stress. Intrusive thoughts. Consistent uncertainty. Overstimulation and also at times under-stimulation. These are the things you're fighting when you work on maintaining balance. Work–life balance isn't a pristine beach that you're always able to navigate to. It's more like the sunset on that beach: you have to set the intention of showing up at the right time and even when you do show up, you don't always get identical results. Rather than pretending there's a simple map to the treasure, here are signs to look out for that indicate that you are or aren't on the right path.

### *When is your balance off?*

Balance is difficult for all remote workers, but the stakes are much higher for digital nomads because we've structured our entire lives around our travel goals. Work–life balance is a buzzword that we all love to hate, but learning to identify the common signs of unbalance will help you to be more attuned to your needs and travel more mindfully with reduced stress. While this conversation usually centres around overworking, work–life balance is a scale, with working on one side and enjoying time off on the other.

## *Overworking*

Overworking often comes from a deeply embedded place. It's encouraged or demanded in many work environments and can be ingrained by your culture and upbringing as well. Rewiring your approach to work to see balance as the highest value is time-consuming.

You may be overworking if these thoughts run through your head:

- I know I'm too busy, but next week/month/quarter things will be different.
- This is only temporary and it's totally worth it.
- Once I get caught up, I'll work less.

This state is caused by the feeling of scarcity, setting an unachievable workload, mismanaging your time, lack of boundaries, malfunctioning systems, lack of alternatives and lack of prioritization. These symptoms are so incredibly common that it's essential to recognize them in yourself and know how to react. Let's look at them one by one.

### Lack of security

The panicked feeling that your income and stability could be pulled out from under you at any time leads you to work harder to either delay that inevitable fall or soften its blow.

Solutions:

- Building up savings as a financial buffer.

- Creating a professional network that will help create future work opportunities for you.

- Increasing your income by raising your rates, negotiating a rise or creating another income stream.

## Unachievable workload

The intended tasks could never actually be completed in the given time. This often stems from a lack of clarity on the steps actually required to complete each task.

Solutions:

- Estimating how long each task will take and time-blocking your schedule.

- Saying no to every new task and opportunity that's not completely essential.

- Reducing your workload through automation, elimination and delegation.

## Mismanaging your time

Time isn't spent on the appropriate tasks or too much time is spent in the wrong area. This can stem from a place of procrastination or a lack of prioritization.

Solutions:

- Recognizing the biggest sources of lost time (example: YouTube) and removing them.

- Removing all non-essential items from your plate.

- Prioritizing your workload.

## Lack of prioritization

Tasks, responsibilities and goals aren't ranked in order of their importance or urgency. You're unable to focus on the most critical tasks first, ensuring that they are completed on time and at the highest-quality level.

Solutions:

- Evaluating your tasks based on impact, importance and urgency.

- Seeking out opportunities to reduce the amount of time each task requires.

- Identifying tasks that can be eliminated altogether.

## Malfunctioning systems

You work efficiently but your systems reduce your productivity. Examples include conversing with teammates in a slow and ineffective manner or manually completing tasks one by one that could be automated or batched.

Solutions:

- Actively seeking opportunities to automate, delegate and eliminate.

- Batching your tasks. Find a task that you do routinely throughout the week or month. Instead of doing this task spread out across time, stack these tasks in one day. After the third time in a row of repeating the process, you'll find a way to reduce the amount of time it takes to complete.

- Asking someone with a similar workload how they manage their work and what standard operating procedures (SOPs) they use.

## Absence of boundaries

Without clear limits or rules around your work activities and expectations, you end up saying yes to every request or opportunity from a client or teammate.

Solutions:

- Understanding that boundaries breed stronger relationships, not weaker ones, and your work and time get more respect when you enforce them being respected.

- Using tools that alleviate difficult conversations. For example, if you have a hard time turning down a client's request for a last-minute meeting, send a calendar booking link with a minimum amount of notice that is required, such as 48 hours.

## Cutoff deprivation

It's unclear when you've finished working. There's no tangible moment that signals the close of your computer and the end of the workday. Instead of being motivated by the carrot, you wait for the inevitable stick: mental exhaustion.

Solutions:

- Scheduling social plans immediately after work.

- Determining a non-negotiable cut-off time, such as 4 pm.

- Visualizing your day with a realistic workload and something to look forward to after work.

While these issues can be independently examined, they're not completely isolated from one another but rather are interwoven in many ways. Scarcity leads to an absence of boundaries. Mismanaging your time comes from a lack of prioritization. All these symptoms are also connected to the other side of the balancing scale: underworking.

## Underworking

The phrase 'I'm so unmotivated' should not exist. Instead, we should be articulating 'I'm so in need of a break' or 'I'm so unstimulated by my work tasks'. Masked as a general lack of motivation, underworking occurs when you're not doing the work that you should be doing. The feeling of being unmotivated is powerful yet largely invisible until you pinpoint the exact problem.

You may be underworking if these thoughts run through your head:

- I physically can't bring myself to work.
- Working isn't worth it when I'm only in [this place] for so long.
- No one will care if I get a bit behind schedule.

When these justifications for underworking become your daily inner monologue, it's time to assess the underlying causes. Underworking can be caused by burnout, spending time on low-impact tasks, boredom or lack of stimulation, tasks being too intimidating, reckoning with failure or being too distracted. Let's look at them one by one.

### Burnout

Exhausting your mental fuel and depleting yourself until you're unable to continue performing at your full capacity.

Solutions:

- Reducing workload to the bare minimum.
- Pivoting to tasks that bring energy back into your work.
- Removing low-impact tasks.

## Doing low-impact work

You feel your hard work doesn't pay off. Despite pedalling harder, you're not arriving at your destination any sooner. Low-impact tasks often feed into the feeling of productivity without ever actually producing results. For example, wanting to publish a blog post but instead you only focus on editing and never actually hit publish.

Solutions:

- Rewording your to-do list (example: *publish* a blog post, not *write* a blog post).
- Measuring the tangible output of specific tasks.
- Reevaluating how these tasks support your larger goals.

## Boredom or lack of stimulation

Tasks are too repetitive or too unchallenging, generating a sense of apathy towards your work. When boredom persists, it's time to consider a shift in the type of work you're doing or a shift in environment.

Solutions:

- Finding a more stimulating work environment.
- Setting a timer and challenging yourself to finish a task within a specific time frame.
- Body doubling (the process of working on a task alongside someone else, either in real life or via Zoom).

## Task intimidation

It's unclear where or how to start a task, so you push by the starting point. Tasks are impossible to complete at once in their form on your to-do list, so they start to feel impossible to complete at all.

Solutions:

- Breaking tasks down into extremely small, manageable steps.
- Dedicating one Pomodoro cycle per day to progressing on intimidating tasks.
- Reminding yourself how this task will help you achieve your larger goals.

## Reckoning with failure

Avoiding a task because your previous attempt was unsuccessful, leading you to postpone getting back up on the horse.

Solutions:

- Articulating what caused failure in the past.
- Finding new ways to achieve your end goal.
- Starting slowly and rewarding yourself for trying.

## Being distracted

Distracted working is a dangerous vacuum where time, motivation and productivity disappear. Without the pressure of your colleagues seeing you work, it becomes particularly important to develop discipline.

Solutions:

- Identifying your distraction go-tos and blocking them if possible. For example, use the Go F*cking Work Google

Chrome extension to block off any webpage of your choosing.

- Using the Pomodoro® Technique and only stopping work during your break periods.

- Turning off notifications during your workday.

Digital nomads face the tricky task of making life balance out work. Achieving that balance isn't easy and it won't happen on its own. Both underworking and overworking cause stress and lead to strains on your mental health, which is why it's so important to learn to identify the symptoms and learn how to troubleshoot.

### How to improve your mental health while travelling

Burnout, stress, anxiety, physical strain, exhaustion – neglecting your mental health has an impressive rap sheet. There are many strategies for improving your mental health as a digital nomad, all of which fall into three categories:

- Physical efforts.

- Organizational efforts.

- Emotional efforts.

Let's start with the area that's easiest to tackle: physical effort. As abstract as mental health may seem on the face of it, our physical surroundings have a massive impact. Here are three opportunities to improve your remote work mental health.

## Have a separate workspace

After surveying my entire network online about their remote work mental health tips, this was the most-mentioned factor that helped with remote work mental health. Who knew having a door to close would become such a commodity? The visual severance of the workspace from the living space has proved to be invaluable.

In particular, separate your workspace from your relaxing, eating and sleeping spaces. This will help with work–life balance, but actually has an even more impactful effect on your focused mental state.

A designated workspace has the benefit of conditioning your mind that this is the place to perform. You speed up the mental process of working by creating routines. By showing up to your focus space and completing a series of expected steps, you mentally prepare for focused work.

Foster a separate workspace to facilitate this state of being 'on' and you'll feel a quick decompression at the end of the workday also. Those living in multi-use spaces such as a one-room Airbnb can still grasp these benefits. Pack your laptop away out of sight after working. Hide work-related apps from your phone and turn off email notifications during non-working hours.

To further this tangible separation, also consider 'commuting' home. When you've finished working, take a walk around the block or a bike ride to clear your head before entering into the relaxation phase of your day. The mental health benefits are even more impactful for your remote work mental health if you don't wait for the end of the day to take breaks like that.

## Take frequent breaks

Learning to pace yourself and implement breaks sounds like it requires a lot of discipline, but you should take comfort in knowing that this is a pass–fail task.

If you commit to a five-minute break for every 25 minutes of working and you don't work during those five 'off' minutes, then you succeeded. Do it for a day and see what a difference it makes. Then try a week. Frequent breaks reduce stress, boost creativity, improve focus and enhance your mood. You need them to succeed with online work. Revel in this win because the next mental health task isn't as straightforward to achieve.

## Develop community

In order to combat the social impact of working online, you must fill the void of colleagues. Even if you work on a remote team and have employees you converse with virtually every day, the amount of interaction is still drastically reduced from that of normal life. Look for communities to join and put socializing on your calendar. In real life (IRL) communities that centre around the remote work experience are plentiful and can be found through platforms such as:

- Coworker, a platform that helps you find a co-working space in upwards of 170 countries
- STROLLÿN, a fusion of Airbnb and co-working where you stay in someone's home and work together

Digital communities are even easier to access. A few options include:

- Location Indie, a digital community of location-independent workers (or aspiring ones) with weekly events online and periodic real-life meetups across the globe (co-founded by Travis Sherry, the creator of the Triangle of Freedom)

- Remotely One, an online community for location-independent workers with a Slack community, real-life events and an app for finding co-working and mentorship opportunities and even dating leads, all within the remote work realm

- LinkedIn, where you can cast your lines and meet a lot of other digital nomads all over the world

Community can also be detached from remote work altogether and centre around a completely different area of your life, such as:

- an interest in movies, books or sports
- physical exercise, hiking or local exploration
- creative outlets such as writing, poetry or music

Loneliness is one of the biggest complaints and mental drains that digital nomads experience. Building a social bubble should be a priority *before* feeling the negative effects.

Developing a separate workspace, joining a Zoom call with other digital nomads and taking breaks are all tangible steps to take to care for your mental health on the road. The next three tips are organizational. I know, no one wants to be told to be more organized. As someone who used to work with toddlers, I've seen firsthand that this resistance to being told to tidy up comes from somewhere very deep and very primitive, but stays on the line. Beyond the natural knee-jerk reaction, I know that the topic of organization can be particularly isolating for neuroatypical remote workers, but there's something here for everyone's mental health.

## Stay ahead of schedule

We've already talked at length about how dangerous letting your work go down to the wire is because of travel uncertainties, but we haven't talked about something even bigger: the negative impact on your mental health. You don't need to be told that procrastination is bad. Has procrastination ever led you to cancel social plans? Or let a task cause infinitely more stress than it needed to? Have you kicked yourself a hundred times for letting things get down to the wire *again*?

Letting a small task get down to the wire and turn into a situation as pressure filled as disarming a bomb is not good for your mental health. If the stick is the only thing that gets you to complete unwanted tasks, then you *must* find your carrot or any other motivational tool to help prevent you from getting into unnecessary high-pressure situations.

## Create systems that work for you

The term 'systems' doesn't just refer to sophisticated workflow software or flowcharts. Systems are the recurring processes that you experience in your work. A system can be as simple as zeroing out your inbox every day or batching a month's worth of LinkedIn content on the last two days of every month.

Systems benefit your remote work mental health because they create patterns and a clear path for success. They can also save you a lot of time, mental fuel and work if they fall into these three categories: automation, delegation and elimination.

These encompass a whole range of processes that make workflow more fluid:

- Automated calendar schedulers such as Calendly.

- Pre-written emails or direct message responses to FAQs.

- Forms on your website that trigger automated emails.

- Social content scheduler.

- Making payments automatically.

Focus on creating clear systems in your business to reduce the number of steps and decisions that fall on your shoulders repeatedly. When set up properly, systems also create achievable tasks, which leads right into point number six.

## Set achievable goals

You wouldn't participate in a scavenger hunt if there wasn't a prize or start learning an instrument without the expectation of someday playing a song. Finish lines matter and so many tasks in business and work become meaningless without them.

Set feasible goals for yourself that you can check off your list. Don't chase goals that are too big or you'll repeatedly fail to achieve them, and remember to be gentle with yourself. Use these guidelines when setting goals specifically to help with mental health:

- Allow more slack than you think you need.

- Track your progress.

- Be honest about why something was or wasn't achievable.

*Can you feel a change in the air?* We've moved from concrete physical tips to a more abstract space. Moving across the scale from physical to organizational to emotional feels reminiscent of decluttering with Marie Kondo. She advises that you save sentimental tidying for last, as it's the most difficult step in the journey.[9]

This task list will be no different. It's easier to rent a co-working space than it is to conquer your personal pitfalls, but you can start making progress with tip number seven.

## Take ownership of your habits

Develop good ones and axe the bad ones. Good news: this can often be done simultaneously.

A very effective way of achieving this is to identify the habits that are most detrimental to your mental health and make reactive good habits that are quantifiable and therefore achievable on a daily, weekly or monthly basis. Do you feel like you're not moving enough? Make sure you get 10,000 steps every day. Struggling with loneliness? Plan a recurring Zoom call with friends every Friday afternoon.

## Don't let things linger

We already brushed up against this remote work mental health tip when we went over the benefits of having a separate workspace, but things linger in more ways than one. I'm talking about emails lingering in your inbox or knowing that you have an uncomfortable conversation somewhere in the near future. You put yourself through the stress of completing a task many times over when you procrastinate.

Have you ever been guilty of a cycle like this?

- You realize that you have to do your taxes.
- It's stressful but it's not due yet, so you postpone it until it's necessary to face it.
- Every week, the taxes to-do looms in your mind and you dread it more with every mental encounter.

- By the time you sit down to do your taxes, it takes five hours. Yet you've spent weeks being affected by this.

This cycle is a brutal, 100 per cent self-inflicted wound. I can say this as an authority because I just did this with my taxes. On the face of it this looks like a problem of procrastination, but in reality the problem is a void of proactivity.

Remote workers must prioritize their to-do lists. If task Z doesn't need to be done for a month, there are naturally tasks A to Y waiting in line ahead of it. But consider identifying the to-dos that will take up unnecessary headspace and reprioritizing them. By moving them to the front of the list, you eliminate days, weeks or months of stress.

## Experience joy after work

It's a truly joyful experience, being able to travel the world while maintaining a career. That's the macro-level joy of this lifestyle, but you also need to find joy in the micro aspects of day-to-day life as a digital nomad. The things that excite you upfront about travelling are going to become commonplace and you need daily sources of joy to maintain a greater appreciation and mindfulness.

Some people will maintain their joy through meditation or hiking. I maintain joy through walks and writing. Bert-Jan feels joy when he sits in the sun drinking his first cup of coffee in the morning or when he closes his laptop and immediately goes outside in the afternoon. It's easy to get caught up in work and neglect other aspects of life, such as hobbies, relationships and self-care. It's even harder for digital nomads because many of those past delights are difficult to access while living life transiently. Joy is as productive and essential as these other work habits and you may find an unexpected source of it on the road: networking.

## Networking as a digital nomad

Rob Palmer walked up to an Irish farmhouse and knocked on the door to ask a question that the people inside had probably never been asked before. 'May I borrow your phone line for my computer?' he enquired with a smile, gesturing at his campervan parked on the road.

It was 1999. The vehicle, which housed Rob, his wife and their four children, was equipped with a bulky computer that relied on a phone line and a dial-up internet connection to access the world wide web. If the strangers said yes to Rob's strange request, he would offer them a small amount of money as a thank-you and lead their phone cord out of their home and in through his campervan window. Some people said no and the search for internet continued. Others said yes and a few even ended up becoming great friends. There were no conveniences built in, with WiFi and internet cafes being years away, but Rob didn't mind the scavenger hunt. Finding access to the internet and logging on to do business for an hour or two a day was a small price to pay for the freedom. That freedom lit a fire that would take Rob and his kids all over the world.

Work had kept Rob tethered to London, but after trialling the remote work lifestyle in his campervan with his family, he realized he could actually work 10 miles outside the city. Then 20 miles and eventually 10,000 when the family moved from the UK to Australia in pursuit of more sunshine and evenings spent barefoot on the beach. His children, now grown, are perhaps the first generation of digital nomad kids. They've all built careers online and his eldest son now works remotely with his partner and their daughter, marking the second generation of children to grow up alongside parents who work online while travelling the world.

The term digital nomad didn't mean anything at the time when Rob drove his first miles down this road. Labels and technology were playing catch-up. Even 20 years later in 2019, he found that many people were uncomfortable with the basic tools of the trade such as video calls. Having a sterling professional reputation and a strong network filled in any gaps.

'I find that you get better at networking the more you do it,' Rob said. 'You have to be prepared to just dive in and chat with strangers.' He followed up this encouragement with a story about a recent business deal that took place at 2 a.m. at a party in the Las Vegas Raiders stadium. Next was a tale of another business deal the next day that resulted from a casual conversation that started in the bathroom. 'You never know when a stranger may become a partner!'

Networking spans both the physical and the digital worlds. All professionals network online, no matter where they're located. Networks based on geographic location are as dated as Rolodexes and digital nomads actually have a leg-up in this area compared to their less digitally inclined professional counterparts.

Professional networks provide tangible benefits to digital nomads. They can foster recommendations and professional endorsements that help build your career. Introductions to clients and hiring managers can be made. Networking provides social support and comradery, as well as mentorship and professional growth opportunities. The opportunity to build a professional network online cannot be overhyped.

Digital networking opportunities can be found in many places online:

- paid community groups (example: Location Indie)
- Facebook groups
- Slack channels
- LinkedIn.

You can also attend networking events in real life if you're willing to travel. Digital nomads who intentionally seek out hotspots such as Bali, Chiang Mai, Lisbon and Medellín will be more likely to find in-person events than those who go off the beaten path. Since becoming a digital nomad, I haven't attended a networking event in real life, but my network has never been stronger thanks to every remote worker's best networking tool: LinkedIn.

That's where I met personal branding specialist and digital nomad Jessie van Breuge, who shared his biggest tip for remote workers to build an effective network: 'Share your unique story through content and proactively reach out to the people who do what you wanna do, or simply people you enjoy spending time (online) with. We're blessed with the abundance of technology, so use it for a good cause.'

## Try this exercise

Log in to LinkedIn (or set up your profile if you don't have one already) and search for posts that mention digital nomadism. Send connection requests with a thoughtful message to digital nomads who are in your industry or a similar one. Having a professional network will pay off in spades and it can be built brick by brick starting today.

# Making yourself futureproof

While you'll find the odd digital nomad whose industry has remained exactly the same over the last 10 years, most of us are dependent on rapidly evolving technology and platforms. The work you'll likely produce will live on the maturing digital landscape and it's a mistake to not expect to see it change. The tools being used and the skills being demanded today may not be popular in a year, so the ability to adapt and stay current with technological changes is crucial for long-term success.

Digital nomads can improve their longevity by:

- developing a specialized skill set that is in high demand
- establishing a positive reputation within their industry
- gathering an audience that they can sell to
- creating a strong professional network.

It's important for digital nomads to be flexible and adaptable to changes in their industries and in the digital world at large. Being future-proof means being able to adapt to changing circumstances and being able to thrive in the always-evolving digital landscape.

The positive news is that not only are digital nomads not disadvantaged in this process, they're usually primed to be more adaptable, resilient and well connected than their location-dependent counterparts. Digital nomads like Rob Palmer and Steven K Roberts have proved that careers can (and will) continue to flourish from just about anywhere.

# Managing your finances abroad

I wasn't broadcasting it to the group, but I was relieved. It was sunset and we were on foot walking towards the border between Honduras and Nicaragua and I was feeling both an excited pull forward towards Nicaragua and a grateful push out of Honduras. That was, until we walked into the small immigration building and began eagerly filling out our border paperwork. The border officials made a demand I was completely unprepared for: pay a border fee of about $10 each, in US dollars only. *They couldn't be serious?* The US dollar wasn't their currency, nor the currency of any of the neighbouring countries. There were no ATMs dispensing US dollars and no currency businesses at the border that offered this. My mind was reeling.

The only thing we could do was turn back into Honduras in the dark and try to find some US dollars in the morning. The relief I'd been feeling was gone and replaced with a familiar anxiety. At the time, Honduras was listed as having the highest murder rate in the world. Despite the brief but perfectly safe experience I had there, that statistic was hard to minimize in my mind as I teetered on the *frontera* in the hot setting sun with some friends I'd met at Spanish school weeks earlier. I leafed through the Honduran lempira in my wallet, burning with the regret of being unprepared, and a memory from a hostel months before floated to the surface. A group of Australian travellers had mentioned how they always ordered US dollars before going abroad and in total surprise I asked them why. '*You've always got to carry US dollars abroad! It's just good common sense, mate.*'

This lack of preparation was particularly searing because it wasn't the first fumble I'd had with money as a digital nomad. In Guatemala, I let my supply of cash run out, only to find that none of the nearby ATMs was functioning. I had to borrow money from friends I'd just met to pay for my hostel. I'd been trying to take out the local equivalent of $200 and despite not receiving anything, the money was still mistakenly withdrawn from my bank account. Standing there at the border, the collective burn of my money mistakes spreading, I swore the next morning I'd take out a pile of Nicaraguan córdobas so I didn't have to worry about money for a nice long while. Little did I know, the huge stack of bills I would withdraw would be stolen out of my wallet in a hostel dorm room just days later. And about a month or so after that, a monkey would steal my wallet in Panama (though I would manage to get it back by scaring the small thief, causing it to thankfully drop the wallet in surprise).

Like a page filled with invisible ink, unwritten rules about travel and money were one by one materializing before my eyes. From how ATMs work to common scams to bank problems, there are many money missteps that you should be aware of before embarking on your digital nomad journey. We're going to walk through all of them together, starting with the steps you should take before you leave to protect yourself financially.

# Preparing your finances before you go

Preparing your finances for travel starts at home and square one of financial success is choosing a bank that suits your needs as a digital nomad.

## *Picking the right bank*

The bank you currently have might not be the bank that will best support your life as a digital nomad. Getting a new bank account abroad, especially if you no longer have a mailing address in your home country, is a process with many hurdles and headaches. Assess and decide on the best bank before you go, looking at these qualities.

### Ability to accept foreign currencies

This ensures that if you start doing work for a company that uses a different currency than that of your home country, you can still receive payments.

### Low or no foreign transaction fees

Find out about the foreign transaction fees charged by your bank for using your debit or credit card abroad. Look for a bank that offers low or no foreign transaction fees to avoid excess charges.

### ATM fee reimbursement

Fees can vary depending on factors such as the bank's policies, the location of the ATM and whether it is an international or out-of-network transaction. The average fee is only a few dollars, but I've seen fees up to $40. If you're travelling in areas where cash is required for all or most daily transactions, these fees add up. See if your bank reimburses you for these ATM fees internationally.

### Outstanding customer service

Consider the availability and quality of customer support provided by your bank. If you'll be travelling across different time zones, having access to reliable customer service, preferably 24/7, is beneficial.

### Fraud protection

Does your bank monitor your account for fraud on your behalf? Investigate how your bank protects you and ask what the process is for getting money back if fraud occurs. Some banks will automatically detect fraud and refund the money to your account without you having to do anything; other banks require you to dispute charges one by one.

### Multiple card options

It's prudent for digital nomads to have at least two bank accounts in the event that one account gets hacked, is inaccessible for some reason or won't be accepted.

## How much money do you need as a digital nomad?

How much money you need to save and should expect to spend as a digital nomad will all come down to your income and approach to budgeting. While most digital nomads who travel long term will move between budgeting tiers, it's helpful to understand where you fall at the beginning of your journey so that you can get a handle on saving, spending and budgeting abroad.

## Budgeting tiers

The four different budget categories are intense budget, frugal budget, budget aware and no budget. Only a small percentage of travellers will fit into the no budget category, but let's start there.

### No budget

Cost is not a factor when planning your travels. Budgetless travellers can travel freely without constraints on how, when and where they go. Digital nomads in this category should pay for all expenses on a credit card with good travel perks to access credit card points that can be traded in for free hotel stays and flights. This practice is called travel hacking: the art of leveraging loyalty programmes and credit card rewards to maximize travel benefits. In order to access pay-outs, you must rack up points on your membership cards or credit cards. The more money you spend, the more you'll have access to these benefits.

### Budget aware

Digital nomads who are willing to pay for a more comfortable experience. This may include regularly eating at restaurants, booking nicer accommodation but looking for discounts, taking clothes to a done-for-you laundry service and renting a car or taking taxis to get around. Budget-aware travellers will be open to peak season and expensive countries and cities, but will balance out these stops with cheaper destinations. Travel hacking should also be utilized.

### Frugal budget

Digital nomads who minimize costs. Common savings include getting budget accommodation, cooking some or most of your own meals, doing laundry at laundromats and taking public transportation. Frugal budgeters will try to avoid peak-season costs and the most expensive countries. Credit card travel perks will be limited because to accumulate points, you must consistently spend money on your credit card. Small purchases and cash purchases, which are the norm in many cheaper travel destinations, make travel hacking at this budget tier (and the next) far less effective.

### Intense budget

Digital nomads who avoid costs. This can encompass doing work exchanges, house sitting, couch surfing or camping instead of paying for accommodation, cooking all your own meals, washing laundry by hand and walking or hitchhiking instead of paying for transit. Intense budgeters will always look to travel in the off-season and seek out countries where their money goes the furthest.

With an understanding of your budget tier in mind, it's time to calculate your monthly expenses abroad.

## *How budgeting will impact your experience*

Budgeting isn't just about restricting your outgoing money: it's a form of security that you provide yourself, which is mighty valuable as a digital nomad where so many normal life securities are unpredictable. A monthly budget provides financial security and in return, peace of mind. Learning to control your expenses might feel uncomfortable at first, but it's a habit that creates extended travel opportunities and reduces stress. It's important to adapt and customize the budget to fit your specific needs and financial situation. Regularly review and adjust your budget as you gain more experience and gather insights about your spending patterns.

# Handling your finances abroad

Holding yourself accountable for your spending is a fundamental pillar of success as a digital nomad and a budget is the best way to do that. Without a well-defined budget, it's easy to overspend and find yourself facing money anxiety. A budget acts as your financial roadmap, guiding your spending decisions and ensuring that you allocate your resources wisely. It helps you prioritize your expenses, identify areas where you can save and stick to your spending goals. By adhering to a budget you gain control over your finances and one of the best tools to help achieve this is financial tracking.

Tracking your finances helps you stay accountable to your goals. This habit helps you gain valuable insights into your spending habits, can detect potential issues early on and make necessary adjustments to maintain a healthy balance. Whether it's through a spreadsheet, budgeting app or dedicated financial software, tracking your finances empowers you to make proactive and data-based choices that support your financial stability as a digital nomad. Start tracking your finances right now to build the muscle and become confident in controlling your finances before you hit the road.

## *Finding your monthly budget*

In order to determine how much money your digital nomad lifestyle will cost, you need to add up all your monthly expenditures. This step is extremely important for travellers with tighter budgets: the lower your monthly income is, the more precise you must be when calculating your monthly costs. Some costs of the digital nomad lifestyle can be minimized, such as accommodation, while others are non-negotiable, such as tourist taxes.

To understand your monthly location-specific expenses, you need to research your monthly living costs in each individual location. As you research destinations and try to estimate your expenses, look primarily for estimates on the cost of accommodation and food. Those prices will impact your day to day more than the price of transportation and recreation.

### Monthly cost warning

There's a common problem that digital nomads encounter during this juncture and that's using the wrong guides to estimate their expenses. Nuance is required as you consume information and advice online. A lot of good advice or insight won't be accurate about every experience. Many cost guides are written by ultra-budget travellers with very low costs and years of experience, who write their guides with the purpose of exhibiting how cheap travel can be. While those people may be telling the truth about their costs (although some others exaggerate), someone new to travel will almost never have access to the exact same level of frugality right away. Some rigorous cost-saving techniques, such as hitchhiking and wild camping, require a level of comfort and travel proficiency that doesn't come overnight.

Extremely frugal travel guides are written for a specific audience: travellers who want to stretch their budget as long and as far as possible. Digital nomads will encounter disappointing surprises if they expect to have access to the exact same experience as these ultra-budget travellers. We all have different needs and some of those needs cost more money: after all, you can't charge your laptop while wild camping on a quiet riverbank in Laos. Likewise, you probably won't find high-speed WiFi and outlets alongside the cheapest cups of coffee in Italy. In fact, in Italy, if you want to sit down at all to drink your coffee, you're sometimes charged double. But thankfully, you can afford to spend more money as you go because your pay cheque comes with you.

Never use an ultra-budget travel guide as your only source of information as you plan your travels and never use one single guide either. It's beneficial to look at multiple cost-of-living estimates as you research that are written by different groups of people. The people who are going to provide the highest-value cost estimates for digital nomads are other remote workers and retirees. Cost-of-living estimates for retirees are often up to date, well thought out and don't cut corners. Correctly estimating and then adhering to your budget is important upfront and will become ingrained in your routine over time, within the first few months of your digital nomad lifestyle. You won't need to complete these steps for every single country you visit over the course of your travels, but you should go through the steps for the first several destinations.

Your costs will fall into one of four categories: living expenses, remote work expenses, travel expenses and recreation expenses.

## Living expenses

All your living expenses, with the exception of insurance, will change depending on your location. Costs like laundry and toiletries will not vary significantly from country to country, but these are still expenses to account for in your calculations. To estimate your living costs, choose the first country you're planning on travelling to as a digital nomad and research how much it costs per night to sleep and eat.

- Accommodation: your accommodation can simply be a bed to sleep in or it can encompass other essential amenities like coffee, cooking, laundry service and a workspace.
- Food: restaurants or grocery stores.
- Recurring personal expenses: laundry (if not included in accommodation), toiletries, etc.
- Insurance: you'll want to consider getting health, travel and liability insurance.
- Savings: Your monthly savings goals should be accounted for, if you have any.

### Remote work expenses

Carefully calculate every recurring expense you have, identifying both monthly and annual costs. Give careful consideration to the costs of using a workspace, subscribing to work platforms (such as Zoom and Google Drive), how much you must set aside for taxes every month if you're self-employed and phone bill costs.

### Travel expenses

The speed at which you travel will impact your travel expenses greatly. Compare a digital nomad who flies to a new destination every month with a digital nomad who flies to a new destination every 90 days and you'll find the taxes, visas and transportation costs are going to be much lower for the slower traveller. The charm of slow travel is so popular with digital nomads that they're sometimes referred to as digital slomads. Consider moving at a slower pace to stretch your budget and gain access to monthly discounts on rentals (sometimes 50 per cent cheaper).

## Recreation expenses

The duration of their travels will often impact a digital nomad's recreation expenses. Remote workers who expect to travel long term will have less of a need to see every waterfall, hike every jungle ruin and inspect every old church. Digital nomads who are travelling for shorter periods of time should budget more for recreation expenses.

## Generating income abroad

Life abroad didn't come at a huge financial cost to Rachel Story; it was actually the exact opposite. It was her economic situation at home in the US that led her to look for financial opportunities in other countries. It was 2009, one of the worst job markets imaginable for fresh university graduates looking for an open door. Rachel and her partner Sasha were crashing with friends as she tried to break into the music industry in Nashville and Sasha tried to find steady teaching work. Rachel took a service job to fill the gaps and the part-time classes Sasha managed to find ended up being eliminated with no notice. They were surviving on food stamps and hustling hard to find a foothold when, on New Year's Eve 2009, their apartment was burgled. 'It's pretty impossible for someone to break into your apartment in Beijing,'

Sasha commented, reflecting on his brief stint as an English teacher there earlier in the year. Rachel was ready for a change. 'Let's go!'

Their landing in China wasn't without turbulence, but within a few months they found their way to a beautiful life. Finally, they had an apartment that they loved, steady jobs that they enjoyed and enough extra money to enjoy some of life's luxuries, like travelling around Asia in their free time. They enjoyed this freedom so much that they saved up $25,000 and after three years of living in Beijing embarked on a 14-month gap year that took them all over the world. Their lifestyle abroad and the skills it taught them improved their financial situation greatly, even when things went wrong (which we'll get to in a minute).

While this doesn't technically fall under the digital nomad umbrella, a closely related cousin to this lifestyle is working abroad. The roles are often language based and opportunities can be explored by searching 'jobs for [language] speakers in [country]'. Finding work abroad is an alternative to living on savings during periods of financial hardship.

## Travel savings

Rachel and Sasha tried to return to their stable lives in China after their gap year abroad, but the stark contrast between full-time travelling and life working at a normal job generated too much friction. They turned to the online world to finance the next iteration of their lives abroad: this time open-ended and fully funded as digital nomads. Sasha and Rachel found work teaching English to kids in China online through a company called VIPKid and it was a steady and enjoyable job for five years. Until one day, when their jobs were outlawed by the Chinese government.

News that shocking isn't something that anyone's ever prepared to hear. Sure, there were rumours of change coming to the online tutoring industry, but they were non-specific. Plus, rules weren't always enforced in China and they didn't expect their work to be completely wiped off the internet. Then one day, with no warning, the hammer dropped and VIPKid announced that all lessons would cease in two weeks. This news came at the very beginning of a two-week US road trip; Rachel and Sasha kicked off some well-earned vacation time with the realization that their jobs would be gone by the time they were back. They'd lost all their lessons with no notice; this was now the second time that this had happened to Sasha as a teacher. VIPKid was once valued at over $3 billion[10] and given the choice of shutting up shop or adapting, Rachel expected the company to adapt. It didn't, at least not in a sustainable way for the teachers who used to rely on the income. But thankfully Rachel had already become adaptable in the online space.

Despite VIPKid being the primary source of income for half a decade, she and Sasha had built multiple income streams online to supplement it, including freelance writing, blogging, YouTube and other language learning platforms. Perhaps just as valuable, they'd also built up a strong network. Rachel collaborated with long-time contacts from Bridge Education Group on updating educational materials, teaching webinars and ultimately developing an entire online course: Succeeding as an English Teacherpreneur. Uncomfortable as it was, Rachel thinks that this shift will ultimately be the best thing that has ever happened to her.

Financial shocks are softened by the professional and financial safety nets that you build for yourself. Your money isn't all equal: some of it will be spent month to month and some of it will hopefully never be spent at all. This is the difference between your monthly outgoings and your savings.

Savings are primarily for when things go wrong:

1 Lost or stolen belongings. Emergency funds can replace stolen items, such as your passport, laptop or phone.

2 Medical expenses. These can include doctor visits, hospital stays or medication (though health insurance is highly advised for these costs).

3 Family or personal emergencies. Costs may include last-minute flights to be with family, sending financial support to loved ones in need or handling unforeseen personal emergencies.

4 Unplanned travel expenses. Travel plans can be disrupted due to various reasons such as flight cancellations, natural disasters or political unrest.

5 Sudden job loss or income reduction. Income loss can happen to anyone – having enough money to cover immediate living expenses is a basic necessity.

On rare occasions, savings can also be there for when unexpected once-in-a-lifetime opportunities arise, though this should never come at the expense of jeopardizing your financial stability.

### Regroup or resolve financial problems

So, how much in savings does a digital nomad need? This answer will depend on how you plan to react to financial distress abroad. Saving categories one to four on the above list will be roughly the same for all remote workers, but category five, 'sudden job loss or income reduction', will split the digital nomad community. Digital nomads fall into one of two categories: those who plan on resolving financial problems abroad (let's call this the *resolution* digital nomad) and those who plan to go home and regroup (let's call this the *regroup* digital nomad). One is not better than the other, but they do come with different financial needs.

Let's examine the regroup digital nomad first. The regroup digital nomad:

- can get by with a smaller savings buffer that covers basic needs and an immediate flight home in the event of job loss

- knows somewhere free to stay back home, such as with family or friends

- has confidence in being able to find income easily and stabilize their financial situation once back home.

That's a relatively light lift when compared with the resolution digital nomad who:

- needs a robust emergency fund that covers several months of all monthly expenses (in addition to savings for lost/ stolen belongings, medical expenses, emergencies and unplanned travel expenses)

- has confidence in being able to pivot and produce new income sources if their income source is permanently lost

- is flexible enough to embrace cost-saving measures and stretch their budget further than normal if the situation demands it.

Do you plan on being a resolution digital nomad or a re-group digital nomad? This answer will likely change as your travels go on. As a brand-new traveller, I was a regroup digital nomad. After my first three months on the road, I was dissatisfied with my job and quit my steady writing gig, pursuing odd freelance jobs and surviving on savings in the interim. I flew to the US from Panama to regroup and try to figure out some of my next steps. I was standing at a number of crossroads and it was therapeutic to work through options from the comfort of my parents' and sister's couches.

While indulging in familiar foods and spending time with family (more time than I'd ever been afforded by a normal job), I worked through some administrative aspects of life that I hadn't left in great shape when I hurried out of Chicago. The storage unit that I had left full of my 'in case I hate travelling' backup life was begging to be cleaned out. The backpack that I had researched for days before buying got replaced with something much better and I repacked it with almost completely different things. I also rearranged some of my money.

In my parents' house months before, I'd left an envelope full of $2,000 cash: a portion of my savings buffer that was protected from my impulsive spending habits. At the time, I didn't trust myself not to spend my entire savings buffer abroad, leaving me with no cash supply to pay for a deposit on my next apartment. I smiled picking up the wrinkly envelope, which had 'next chapter' written on it in marker pen. A few months on the road had changed me. I felt more in control and more confident, so I deposited that stack of ten- and twenty-dollar bills into my bank account, knowing that my next chapter wouldn't necessarily be in the US anyway. That month spent regrouping before picking travel back up in Colombia was invaluable to me on an emotional, financial and preparedness level. Years later when my income took a hit, I was steadier and able to resolve my problems abroad.

You can never be completely confident about what your answer to this question will be down the road, but it's prudent to explore the hypothetical situation of losing your income source in the next six months and think through the emergency response. Doing so will help you feel more grounded and will guide you through establishing your savings threshold now and starting to immediately and aggressively put money aside.

## Generating your travel savings

It was a bad day to be hungover, but there I was: a scalp covered in jelly, electrodes stuck all over my wet hair, chin and forehead fixed in a holder, staring at a screen in front of me that was tracking my eye movement as I completed exercise after exercise. Instead of spending my Saturday on my couch eating scrambled eggs and breakfast potatoes covered in ketchup (the way God intended for hungover Saturdays to be spent), I was instead doing an EEG experiment for $60 at the University of Chicago. The entire process would last about three hours, with a wad of cash and a plate of potatoes at the end of the tunnel. Between sessions, I asked one of the researchers if he had other studies going on that I could participate in. He laughed a little as he replied, 'Really looking for some extra money, huh?' while adding more jelly to my scalp cap.

I suppose my air of desperation was palpable. The core of my work week took place as a marketer Monday to Friday and I brought in extra money at weekends with university experiments, babysitting and selling plasma. Maybe it did look a little crazy from the outside, but I was in overdrive mode trying to save money for full-time travelling. Truthfully, I was terrible at budgeting and not very disciplined with shopping, so I was convinced there was no such thing as too much financial preparedness and I was right. A well-funded savings buffer is one of the greatest assets an aspiring digital nomad can develop. Generating it comes from two different places: increasing income and deflating lifestyle costs. Let's talk about lifestyle deflation first.

## Lifestyle deflation

Lifestyle deflation is the act of reducing the amount of money that your entire lifestyle costs. It's the solution to lifestyle inflation, which is often a creeping and invisible or even encouraged increase in monthly spending. It's a story as old as time: with a new job comes a higher salary and a more expensive wardrobe and a bigger apartment and maybe a nicer car. Dinner bills become bigger and more frequent and you enjoy picking up the tab for friends at the bar. The next thing you know, all the extra money left over at the end of the month is gone.

We can bring that extra money back by implementing the opposite system: intentionally pulling back the costs of your entire lifestyle. This is one of the most effective ways to start building your digital nomad savings right away. On the scale of lifestyle costs, you have essential expenses on one side and optional expenses on the other. Optional expenses are the easiest to cut, so we'll start there and then work our way to essential expenses. Follow these steps now to put more money into savings and maintain these habits on the road to lower your ongoing costs as you go.

## Reduce your exposure to advertising

Work through your email inbox today and unsubscribe from all promotional emails. Unfollow accounts that tempt you to spend money on social media. With the exception of travel gear, your shopping habit should end right away. Unnecessary shopping wastes money and beyond that a digital nomad who's about to downsize into a backpack or suitcase needs very little anyway. Don't spend money on things that you'll just put into storage or give away in six months.

## Wait a month to make every purchase

If you must buy a new item, enforce a one-month waiting period and don't allow yourself to make any impulsive purchases. Side effects include forgetting that you ever wanted to buy something, finding a solution that you already own, borrowing the item from somebody else or discovering it second hand. After a month, if you still have a need for the item, you can make the purchase with confidence, knowing it's not an emotional or impulsive decision.

## Minimize recurring purchases

By critically examining recurring expenses and making conscious trims, you can free up more funds for travel experiences and long-term financial goals. On a smaller scale, this refers to monthly subscriptions, memberships, software purchases, etc. On a larger scale, this includes rent, car payments, insurance and beyond. Minor monthly savings can come from quitting premium apps and memberships that you hardly use. Major monthly savings can come from getting housemates, moving in with a family member temporarily and trading your car for other means of transport. If you've already secured a remote income source, a particular amount of depth is available to you in this savings area.

### Initiate a strict weekly budget for food

This budget should cover groceries, eating out and beverages such as coffee and alcohol. This is a special lifestyle deflation item because its importance goes far beyond the actual money saved. Being able to successfully stick to a chosen budget is going to drastically impact your financial stability on the road and your food spending is the best place to strengthen this muscle. By establishing a weekly budget, you have a new opportunity to improve and succeed at budgeting every seven days.

These lifestyle deflation tactics will help slow the rate at which your money goes out and are extremely influential on your ability to save for travelling. Pair these efforts with an income increase and you'll be shocked by the savings you're able to achieve.

### *Income increase*

On the other end of the savings spectrum from lifestyle deflation is increasing your income. You can either focus on increasing the income that you already get from your job or you can bring in new income streams. Side hustles can be done locally, such as dog walking, childcare and tutoring, or they can be digital. Practically any service can be turned into a side hustle online and some remote workers even work two full-time jobs one after another Monday to Friday. This is called being overemployed and while it's an incredibly effective way to build up your savings buffer, any aspiring nomads who choose to take on entire second jobs must pay close attention to their energy levels and mental health. I recommend picking a savings number that you wish to hit with your side hustle to avoid burnout and keep morale high. It's easier to pick up odd jobs at the weekend if you know you're getting closer to hitting your savings buffer threshold.

A balanced blend of travel prep straddles both lifestyle deflation and income increase, though some will be exempt from one or both of these. Most people, but not everyone, will find ample savings in deflating their lifestyle costs. For example, if you currently live rent-free with your parents, you will probably have limited opportunities to deflate your lifestyle costs. Likewise, if you've already maxed out the number of hours you're able to work per week, you probably can't bring more income in. There's no single solution, but explore the options with an open mind to see how you can reach your savings goals quickly and efficiently.

## Common money problems while travelling

Almost every digital nomad has a story about running out of money. Not running-out-of-money running out of money, but running out of cash in a place where cash is all that matters and what's the difference at that point? If you can't pay for your meal or bus ticket or whatever else your immediate circumstances necessitate, you're put into emergency problem-solving mode. And that usually ends up being expensive.

You can blame an ATM being empty or being pickpocketed or only having a Mastercard when all they take is Visa, but the common thread in many of these stories is that all countries have unwritten rules about money. The further you go off the beaten path, the more unwritten rules there will be and the less able or willing to compromise people become.

Every rule can't be accounted for, but familiarize yourself with the common headaches of travelling abroad to avoid expensive and compromising situations.

Before you go, research:

- whether credit cards are accepted and which ones (though this is often unreliable – more on this in a moment)
- whether or not tips are required
- if bargaining or negotiating is a normal practice
- common scams.

Find answers to these questions to develop a location-specific set of guides for yourself and follow the following general best practices for handling your money abroad.

## Cash best practices

While digital payments are prevalent in many countries, cash remains an important aspect of international travel. By following these guidelines, you can navigate cash transactions with confidence and enjoy your travel experiences without landing yourself out of money and out of luck.

### Always carry cash

Cash is everything in many parts of the world; this can be a result of local culture or lack of access to digital payment infrastructure. From bribes to surprise cash-only tourist taxes and everything in between, unexpected cash needs can and will arise anywhere. As a result, you can never afford to run out of cash. While it may be tempting to spend every last yen or rand before crossing borders, it's irresponsible to do so. Always have cash for:

- bathrooms
- tips
- border fees
- tourist taxes
- bus and train terminal fees
- surprise fees or bribes
- broken ATMs (therefore a delay in getting more cash)
- emergencies. From a safety perspective, you should always have some cash on hand to hail a cab if you suddenly feel unsafe where you're walking or to pay for a hotel unexpectedly.

## Break big notes right away

When an ATM gives you large bank notes (bills), immediately change them them for coins or smaller notes as small vendors might not accept them. You can try to do this at a bank or a larger store.

## Don't accept tarnished notes

Check notes for tears or vandalism before accepting them. In some countries, such notes are unusable and small vendors will sometimes give them to foreigners just to get rid of them; then it becomes the foreigner's problem when they try to pay with it later. Show the cashier the tear or writing and hand it back.

## Carry some emergency money in US dollars

Only take small, untarnished notes.

### ATM and digital payment best practices

Even though you may not think twice about withdrawing cash at home, in many countries it's a normal part of life for digital nomads. Let's explore the best practices for handling ATMs abroad, including tips for currency exchange, safety and protecting your digital assets.

## Be aware that ATMs sometimes run out of money

The frequency of this varies by country. In an area where this often happens, locals will often be aware of which day the ATMs are refilled but you won't be when you first arrive. Pay attention to patterns if you stay long term in a country where this happens.

## Use ATMs inside banks rather than on the street

Not all outdoor ATMs are problematic, but those inside banks provide more protection. Banks have security and the odds of the machine being tampered with are lower. Use these machines during the day and never at night to minimize your odds of being robbed.

## Have multiple types of bank cards

It's wise to have access to two different bank card types, for example a Visa and a Mastercard, in case one can't be processed. This rule doesn't just apply to countries with less access to digital infrastructure; it's not uncommon to come across cash registers with all the common banking logos listed yet your Visa is rejected or your Mastercard just won't go through. Having a second card on hand is a real asset.

## Choose ATM currency wisely

Reject the currency exchange rate offered by the machine when withdrawing cash and instead always withdraw and pay in local currency. You're often charged more when the money is converted from your bank's currency to the local currency.

## *Safety best practices (and surprises)*

A crime-avoidance mindset is a daily part of digital nomad life and there are specific ways to safeguard your finances from crime.

### Talk to other travellers

Every destination has unwritten rules about how to avoid being scammed or robbed. The most universal rule is to not take cash out at an ATM after dark to avoid being robbed, but there is also local information about everywhere you'll travel. Ask other travellers where they're taking money out and whether they've had any problems and you'll unearth an incredible amount of information and advice.

### Store your cash in multiple locations

From your day-to-day wallet to your travel documents wallet to the bottom of your 'maybe I'll wear these later' shoes, your cash should never all be stored in one place. Split it between bags, and most importantly only carry a small amount on you per day. There's no need to carry more than your daily budget of money at one time. That way, if you lose your money or your bag gets stolen, you've only lost some and not all your cash supply. This same principle applies to carrying around multiple credit cards: only take with you what you actually need every day.

## Separate money in your bank account

Debit card theft, whether physical or digital, is something to proactively protect yourself against. Part of your protection comes from choosing a bank with fraud detection and avoiding suspect ATMs and another part comes from within your bank account. Separate the money in your bank account so that the majority of your savings is inaccessible at a moment's notice. Only keep what you realistically need available in the spending part of your bank account, for example $200. Then if your card is stolen, any purchase above $200 will be rejected and you're automatically protected from large purchases that drain your account.

## Never use public WiFi for banking purposes

Only access your banking information or any password-sensitive information on private WiFi. Using a VPN will protect your connection further.

## Check for visa requirements concerning money

Some countries require proof that you have a certain amount of money in your bank account before they will grant you a visa. Prepare for this situation before you arrive as it may take several days to transfer money between locations.

## Accept that prices may change

Fixed prices are cultural, not universal. As a foreigner, you may be charged more than the locals for the same product. You may also see prices change, where the exact same bowl of soup costs five different amounts on five different days.

All of these tips will help you hold onto your money while living as a digital nomad, but there are also techniques and lifestyle changes that will help you routinely spend less.

## Saving money while travelling

My parents offered to order a cab, but our money-saving habits were a comfort to Bert-Jan and me after years of travelling. 'We enjoy the walk!' we insisted as we headed out the door with Google Maps in hand and left my parents to settle into the Airbnb in the coastal surf town of Nazaré, Portugal. The task was straightforward: go to the shop for some basic groceries and then head to pick up pizza. It was a warm autumn night, perfect conditions for a walk, and I estimated we would return in about an hour.

'It feels like we've been going downhill forever,' I said after a while, noticing that we'd been walking steadily down a continuous steep slope. It was pitch black and I couldn't visually confirm, so my mind moved on from the thought. By the time we'd stocked up at the shop and picked up the two extra-large pizzas, we were carrying quite the load and were eager to get back to the Airbnb where my parents were waiting. 'The walk back is only 15 minutes,' I thought, refusing to let myself regret the cab rejection. We faithfully followed Google Maps' directions, not thinking much of the zigzagging route laid out for us. Fifteen minutes had passed, but on the map it didn't look as though we'd moved very far at all. My arms felt like they might fall off from carrying the stuffed shopping bags and my legs begged for a break. Google Maps had taken us along a scenic walking route that scaled a cliff.

After countless pauses and complaints (from me, never Bert-Jan, who is made of steel), we arrived back at the Airbnb ready to collapse on the couch with wobbly legs and devour the pizza that was now half cold. The next day, the four of us set off to see the sights and we saw that we'd walked up a hill so steep that it had a funicular to transport people up and down the 1,042 foot track. 'Oh my gosh, you should've taken a cab!' my mother said and she was right. But this wasn't the first time we'd shot ourselves in the foot being cheap, and despite having enough money to pay for simple luxuries like a cab to the shop, it wouldn't be the last.

Your relationship with money and the things you spend it on will change as you travel. Your income may change as well, forcing a shift in how you spend your pay cheque. Even if you begin your digital nomad lifestyle as a budget traveller, with experience, improved budgeting and financial discipline and potentially splitting costs with friends or partners along the way, it's often possible to reduce your costs further if the situation necessitates it. For digital nomads who fall into the intense budget, frugal budget and budget-aware categories, there are many habits and lifestyle choices that can help drastically reduce outgoing money every month. These tricks don't need to be unilateral laws of your lifestyle, but they can be available to you when money gets tight or during seasons of savings.

There are five main ways to spend less money as a digital nomad:

- **Accommodation.** Consider moving from hotels into hostels or from Airbnb into house-sitting or work exchanges. Book accommodation that covers multiple cost areas. Being able to cook, work and do laundry from your accommodation is going to reduce costs drastically.

- **Meals**. Cook at home and eat like a local. Eating out in touristy restaurants adds up, but street food and the menu of the day can be just as cheap as buying ingredients from the shop. Embrace the art of cooking your own meals and eating what's cheap locally and in season. Limit your spending when buying beverages such as coffee and alcohol.

- **Travel speed**. Slow down. Slow travel is cheaper and therefore more sustainable. Long-stay discounts and the absence of travel costs such as flights can help you cut your budget drastically. Embrace slow travel in your day-to-day tasks as well and if an errand takes less than an hour, walk or take public transport instead of taking a cab or renting a car.

- **Consult your budget**. Look back at what you spent your money on over the last 90 days and seek areas to cut costs that aren't covered in the above categories. A clear understanding of your money helps you make informed decisions, not emotional ones.

- **Get advice from locals and other travellers**. Find advice locally and online on how to save money if you get into a difficult situation abroad. There are online travel Facebook groups that cover most regions of the world – ask for advice and recommendations.

Now that we've explored various strategies to save money as a digital nomad, let's turn to an equally important aspect of managing your finances: paying taxes. Understanding your tax obligations as a digital nomad is crucial to maintain financial compliance and avoid any legal issues down the road. While the topic is about as pleasant as having food poisoning on a long-distance bus ride without air conditioning, it's important and I promise I'll keep it brief.

# Taxes

The conversation about digital nomads and taxes can be either short or long. Let's start with the short: travel to whichever countries you like and find a tax accountant in your home country who specializes in digital nomads to file taxes annually on your behalf. If you can't find one, settle for a tax accountant who specializes in expatriates and make sure they understand your situation.

The longer conversation about digital nomad taxes revolves around choosing your foreign destination with the purpose of reducing how much money you pay in taxes. The laws surrounding digital nomad visas are evolving rapidly as countries scramble to tap into the global boom of remote working and these often come with appealing tax provisions. While this generally involves getting residency or registering a business based in a specific foreign tax haven, there's a lot to be explored on a nomad tax map and you may be surprised to see which countries offer the greatest tax opportunities.

Taxes can feel like an unsavoury part of planning your digital nomad lifestyle, but with a few basic pieces of insight, you can feel confident navigating the red tape.

## General things to consider

Taxation is easiest for employed individuals, as your employer will typically withhold part of your income for taxes automatically. Self-employed individuals will have to handle this process independently, with considerations for what country their business is registered in, what country or countries their income comes from and where they're currently residing.

Just like the average at-home citizen who looks to reduce how much they owe in taxes, digital nomads look for legal loopholes that can save them money on their taxes, some of which are more influential than others. For example, Americans are compelled to file and pay taxes no matter where they live in the world. This is called citizenship-based taxation and it's utilized only by the US and Eritrea. Americans staying in some foreign countries long term will have to pay local taxes in addition to US taxes, which is a situation called double taxation. Many tax treaties exist to help combat this and it's something to research if you plan on staying abroad long term, partially with residence visas or digital nomad visas.

From navigating the complexities of international taxation to leveraging tax benefits and available deductions, free internet resources aren't enough to rely on. Filing your taxes is not an area to cut corners to save money. It's an annual expense that can be small or medium sized (depending on your accountant's fee) or it can be higher if mistakes are made. Working according to online advice and trying to DIY your taxes contains an inherent risk, as laws, regulations and tax treaties never finish evolving.

Like all aspects of a new lifestyle, money is something to be neither feared nor avoided, just understood.

# When things go wrong

For years, Travis Sherry built his travel blog, Extra Pack of Peanuts, alongside his day job as a high school teacher in Japan. Finally, the day came: Travis and his wife Heather left their jobs and set out to become full-time travel bloggers and digital nomads. Travis purchased a brand-new MacBook Pro for this exciting chapter and embarked on weeks of travel through Singapore, Indonesia and India. But on the very first day of the trip, he accidentally left his MacBook Pro behind in Singapore. A friend there mailed it to another friend in India and Travis thought that he and his computer would arrive at roughly the same time. After weeks of travelling in Asia, the computer never arrived and Travis and Heather flew to the US computerless.

The MacBook Pro was held up in customs where officials were hoping for a bribe to release it and even once that computer was in the right hands in India, it was too expensive to mail it to the US. But months later, the parents of a friend were travelling to India and through an enormous chain of networking, the computer was delivered back to Travis. After five months without a computer as a full-time travel blogger, Travis had his MacBook Pro back in his hands. Then that very same day, a cup of coffee was spilled directly on the keyboard and fried the essentially unused computer beyond repair.

Travis laughed as he told me this story, a telltale sign that significant time has passed. There are a lot of social measurements for how long it takes to get over a breakup and there's some similar invisible metric for how long it takes to get over an expensive travel mistake. For digital nomads, I think it's somewhere between the time when you're trying (and failing) to not think about the money lost when you look at your bank account and the first time you tell the story at the bar for laughs.

Every adventure will have problems, both of the stressful and the expensive persuasions. After a little bit of travelling, you'll be able to add 'problem solving' as a skill on your résumé because you're going to put out fires that you didn't even know could exist. The confidence boost is surprising. So are many of the headaches.

While it may sound like general travel savvy, advice around travel safety and accident avoidance is as important to your career as anything else that you'll do as a digital nomad. Your income and stability are jeopardized if your laptop is broken, stolen or you're too unwell to work. The digital nomads who are able to travel the longest are the ones who care the best for their physical safety, their wellness and the safety of their electronics. How you handle these situations will be an important factor in how you enjoy this lifestyle and how your career develops while travelling. We'll examine the common concerns that digital nomads will have to navigate and specific ways to proactively avoid problems with your technology and health, plus encounters with crime.

You've heard the expression 'anything that can go wrong will go wrong'. That actually doesn't apply to travel because things will go wrong that you didn't realize were possible. Here's where you should start.

## Tech problems abroad

A small gap between my computer screen and the plastic border that frames it catches my eye. I'm at my apartment in the Netherlands, sipping a fresh cup of coffee on my couch, writing an article for a client. *Did that just happen or am I just noticing it?* I have work to do; I keep writing. Within two hours, the gap has grown from the bottom corner across the entire right-hand side of the screen. All of a sudden a shift in tension causes the screen to lift up on the right side, ripping the metal hinge out of its normal resting place. My jaw drops in shock and my heart starts racing. I instinctively hit my computer's power button and then cautiously close the screen.

There's a sickening crack. A piece of plastic falls out and suddenly I'm able to see inside my laptop. I'm in such a state of surprise that I have almost no words to explain what happened to Bert-Jan, who was sitting only a few feet away but missed this whole catastrophic event. The woman at the repair store assures me this is a lot more common than you'd expect. Two weeks later, my computer is returned with a new screen. Peeling the protective plastic layer off doesn't have the same satisfaction that it would have normally had because now I've figured out how my computer broke, and I wasn't as much of a victim as I initially believed.

A few weeks prior to this incident, I was travelling in Spain and Portugal and I slowly bent my laptop in half. I stuffed all my gear into a carry-on-sized backpack, just like I'd done countless times before. But this computer was relatively new, and bigger than any other laptop I'd had in the past. Still I pulled *up* on the bag and pushed *down* on the laptop to make it fit into this non-existent space. The continual pressure set off an invisible chain of events: the screen was bent slowly for weeks, loosening the glue, until one day enough tension was lost for the plastic frame to release itself from the screen. Now, I can't guarantee that this will happen to you, but I'd bet my newly repaired laptop screen that something equally detrimental will happen to your tech if you travel for long enough.

## Most common problems

Reflect on your own history with electronic devices: how many times have you needed to take something to a repair shop or get a replacement? Add the compounding effects of being toted from state to state or country to country and you'll likely need to replace things even sooner than you did back home. Here are the common laptop problems that occur on the road, placed in order of increasing severity.

### Keys stop working

Whether the keys are sticking or just losing sensitivity, the integrity of your keyboard will weaken over time. The underlying problem may be expensive, but the short-term solution is affordable and easily accessible: get an external keyboard. This can be Bluetooth or USB and can be found almost anywhere, even at second-hand stores.

### Lost or broken computer charger

Computer chargers get lost and stop working. At home, this is a minor inconvenience; you can order any charger online and have it delivered in two shakes. But access to specific brands and models of chargers is regional and your computer may not be common in whatever part of the world you're travelling in. If you can't find a replacement charger, you'll need to be prepared to buy a new laptop.

## Water or environmental damage

Sand, 100 per cent humidity, spilled water – minimize whatever environmental damage you can for your laptop. Never leave open glasses or bottles next to your laptop and don't eat over your computer. Don't work around sand and get your laptop cleaned once a year.

## Drops and falls

Always keep your laptop in your own hands and make it a rule to always set your bag down on the ground; never drop it. Drops and falls will be minimal if you are the only one who handles your bag carrying your laptop. More on this in a minute.

### *How to prepare*

'You'd be surprised how often it happens,' punctuated most of Tim Beck's stories, which all sounded like episodes of 'A Thousand Ways to Die: Computer Edition'. Tim is the owner of Computer Medix, a computer repair store in my hometown in Pennsylvania. The laptop that I'd been using abroad for five years started severely malfunctioning in Greece and Tim brought it back to life, then was gracious enough to share his advice with me on laptop care for travellers.

I pulled my computer out onto my lap to take notes as we talked and Tim winced. 'A laptop isn't *actually* meant to be used on your lap.' And just like that, I was about to change the way I used my computer. Here's Tim's advice for digital nomads.

## Don't use your laptop on a soft surface

Routinely using a laptop on soft surfaces shortens its lifespan because the internal components overheat. This often causes slow damage over the course of months or years and can happen without you realizing it. If you must use your laptop on your lap (or another soft surface), place something hard like a book in-between.

## Respond to fan errors

If you get a fan error, shut down your computer immediately and take it to a repair shop right away. While a fan malfunction might not cause your computer to stop working immediately, the internal components of your computer might be slowly melting.

## Don't enter sensitive data on public WiFi

Anytime you use WiFi, you're opening up your computer's connection to other users on the same WiFi network. Scammers seek out crowded public networks, such as airports, and look for computers with vulnerabilities to exploit. Protect your data by minimizing the amount of time you spend on these networks and don't enter your passwords.

## Open and close your computer from the centre of your screen

Holding the corner of your screen as you open and close your laptop torques the hinge. Laptop hinges are steel, but they're mounted in plastic, which is slowly damaged by thousands of twists. To preserve your laptop hinges, always open and close from the centre of the screen.

## Don't let other people handle your electronics

Take a carry-on-size backpack (also known as a day bag) that fits all your most valuable things and never give it away to anyone, for any reason. Don't check it on a flight, throw it in storage on a train or let it be strapped on the roof rack of a bus. Be prepared to be firm, no matter how much someone insists they handle your bags for you. Out of politeness, I once let an insistent Airbnb host carry my backpack for me, only for her to drop it dead on the ground with the most sickening *thud* once we got into the room.

## Put every piece of tech in a waterproof casing

Don't buy 'water-resistant' laptop or tablet cases. Water resistance is too vague; you need plastic that is designed to keep water out completely. Pack a large Ziplock bag that fits your laptop and any other electronics. Placing your laptop in a Ziplock should become a part of your routine every time your laptop gets packed into your bag. A Ziplock protects your laptop from weather, other liquids inside your bag and unexpected water encounters, like unknowingly setting your bag down on a damp floor.

## Invest in a quality laptop

Does your laptop suit all your needs? It should be steadfast and reliable for your work and it also needs to provide your creature comforts. If you like to play games, make sure your laptop has a good GPU (graphics processing unit). Use your laptop to fill the void of electronics back home that can't be brought along for the ride. Whatever you get needs to be a fast, completely reliable machine that can be repaired when issues occur.

### How to react

On a micro level, moments of tech crisis are situations to problem solve and survive. But on a macro level, the way you react to these crises is an opportunity to prove to your team, manager or clients that you are just as capable and reliable as non-remote workers. These moments will be judge and jury and will determine the verdict of this lifestyle to your professional circle.

There are five primary steps to resolving a broken laptop:

**1** Take computer to repair shop.

**2** Get estimate of when repairs will be done.

**3** Determine who you need to inform.

**4** Send clear and calm notifications.

**5** Close conversation loop with team after laptop is repaired.

This may have an air of common sense to it, but it's a great comfort to have a checklist when you see your income and lifestyle thrown into limbo. There's no denying the stress of laptop malfunctions, but pause the feelings of guilt. Don't apologize unless it negatively affects someone, and send calm and brief emails.

Spare your boss unnecessary details like 'I'll have to take six buses and travel for two days in hopes of finding a computer shop with the parts I need'. These aren't moments to highlight the exotic nature of your lifestyle; with any problem you face, being relatable will be an asset. Not everyone has had their computer charger chewed through by a sea turtle before, but everyone *has* had computer problems. Avoid emotionally charged language and don't pass any stress onto your team.

## Set realistic expectations

It's important to never leave anyone wondering 'Will they get this done on time?' If you're not going to make a deadline or you think there's a risk you may fall short, be very forthcoming with that information. The more notice you give about potential schedule setbacks, the better, and be cautious in estimating when you'll be back online. It's better to under-promise and overdeliver on your availability than the other way around, so always overshoot how long you expect the problem to take.

Factor in local culture when you make this estimate. Observe a country's relationship with time: do restaurants open at the time listed on their door? When you're told to wait for five minutes, does it turn into two hours without an apology or explanation? This fluid and more flexible approach to time frames is called polychronic time and it's jarring when coming from a monochronic time culture. It's important to gauge *your* expectations so that you can gauge your *team's* expectations as accurately as possible.

While tech problems seem bad (and they are), they don't necessarily need to make you *look* bad. Use moments of crisis to communicate your proactivity organization and problem-solving skills to your team and lay out the next steps for them to react to. Let's break down those qualities using the example of a YouTube video producer with a broken computer. Here's how they could use this crisis to highlight their skills:

- **Proactivity**. 'We were already three weeks ahead of schedule, so this delay won't impact the campaign at all, but I wanted to give you a heads up that I may be slower to respond while my laptop is being repaired.'

- **Organization.** 'If you want to look at any of the content while I'm offline, you can find everything in the [X] folder organized by campaign and labelled pending, approved or published.'

- **Problem solving.** 'We can postpone the videos for the next few days since none of them is time sensitive and then I will spread them out next week instead. Or I can let [team member] know where everything is in the files and ask them to publish the videos. What are your thoughts?'

In your communication, make it clear where the responsibility will fall. Instead of saying 'this can't be published today, we can publish it next week instead', say '*I* can publish it next week instead'. Take responsibility for your tasks and leave teammates with the feeling that they know how things are being handled. If someone needs to respond right away in order for you to act accordingly, put 'time sensitive' in the subject line of the email and give them a time frame for when you need a response. The worst thing you can do is send panicked, unclear emails where your teammates have to decipher what your broken laptop means for them.

Highlight your proactivity organization and problem solving: this is the recipe for a professional, clear and level-headed response to tech crises abroad. Once your problems are resolved, let your team know that you're back online in working order with a simple email that reiterates any changes or moved workload and acknowledges the work they did to bridge your tech gap. If tech breakdowns become common, consider some IT training so that you can handle basic troubleshooting yourself. Google offers free Google IT Support Certificates which will give you basic troubleshooting skills.

## Health problems abroad

One day in Guatemala, a small red splotch appeared on my right palm. *Is this new or am I just noticing it? If it's something to actually worry about, it'll become apparent.* It quickly spread across my hands and then, soon after, my feet. The skin on my feet became weak and broke open easily. Nervous but not wanting to overreact, I jokingly started calling it trench foot and Googled fungal infections. I bought cream at a local pharmacy and retired my sandals, buying a pair of protective trainers instead at a mall in Managua, Nicaragua.

When FaceTiming with my parents, who are both nurses, I described my feet and asked them for their recommendations. They insisted on looking at my feet before giving advice, but I refused and brushed it off because I knew what they would say: come back to the US and go to a doctor. Within a month or so, I was back in Chicago for other reasons and went to a walk-in medical clinic first thing. It took me a long minute to slowly remove my shoe and peel back my sock. The pain was so bad that walking was extremely difficult. The doctor refused to treat it and sent me to a dermatologist.

Months of pain, Google searches and concerned texts from my parents all came to a quick and decisive end. 'Eczema,' the dermatologist confidently diagnosed in Pennsylvania a week later. I was given steroid cream and the improvement overnight was so significant that I was already prepared to act like this whole thing never really happened. My mother was there with her reliable doses of reality: 'You have to really learn to take care of this or you'll be right back in this exact situation.' Managing my eczema has been a regular part of my life for years now and my family still calls it trench foot. But my travels aren't at risk or jeopardized because of it.

Pushing through health issues isn't nearly as strong, smart or *live-in-the-moment-y* as it seems. A little wisdom (or enough tissue damage) makes this apparent. In order to enjoy your travels, you have to be well enough to leave your room and see something. The scares and health concerns aren't Instagram-worthy moments, but they are the reality of travelling long term.

Health is not a result of choice or virtue. The majority of health is decided by luck, fate or God, however you philosophize it. A small percentage is a result of intentional choice and that's what you can and should prioritize while travelling. It will move mountains for your digital nomad experience. Here's where you should start.

### Most common problems

Travel, while good for the soul, is demanding on the body. With some of these demands, your body will rise beautifully to the occasion. As you heave on your pack and inch your way from town to town, you'll find yourself growing stronger. Feeling more energized. A sedentary lifestyle, now a small dot far behind you in the rear-view mirror. This side of travelling is pure bliss and I know I personally have yet to tire of being told how healthy and tanned I look.

Behind those gains will lie pains of varying degrees. The average traveller will encounter more blisters, insect bites and sunburn than life in a cubicle could ever bring. You'll come to quantify things that you've never even thought about before, like the number of mosquito bites on your body at one time (my personal record: 31). If you have a delicate constitution, you should brace yourself for the impact of these demands. Most ailments are temporary, though some aspects of your health may remain altered long term.

In particular, many travellers who've had digestive issues recall that their stomach didn't go back to normal. I've heard stories from travellers covering the entire digestive spectrum – from contracting giardia to just having bad indigestion, many travellers have uttered the same sentiment: '*My stomach was just never the same after that.*' Personally, I used to boast about my iron stomach, until I reacted to something in Peru. This set off days of bloated, painful digestive discomfort, followed by a few weeks of feeling off and when the dust finally settled, my iron stomach was now sensitive and has been ever since.

Reaching for your familiar over-the-counter remedies will not be a reliable option abroad as pharmaceuticals vary widely from country to country. Most bumps along the road won't require medical attention, but it's good to be aware of the common causes of health problems while travelling and how to react if necessary.

## Unusual foods

Digestive issues are the source of most health-related travel stories. There's a spectrum of causes, with unusual foods being on the innocent end. Unusual foods won't necessarily make you violently sick, but they can leave you feeling bloated, constipated or just *off*. If new foods are causing problems for your digestive system, book accommodation with a kitchen and cook for yourself, then eat out occasionally to slowly help your system adjust.

## Food poisoning

Food poisoning can happen anywhere, but you'll be more prone to it with some countries and foods. Read online if there are any specific risks to be aware of in the countries you're travelling to. In places with street food, minimize food poisoning risk by eating at popular food stalls. It may be tempting to pick the food stall with the shortest queue, but a food stall with only a few customers has food sitting around longer (often in the heat). A long line of patrons means that food is being rotated more quickly and is fresher. Eating vegetarian food will also minimize your risk of food poisoning.

## Dehydration

While dehydration isn't an issue that puts most travellers in hospital, it does have an enormous effect on your overall feeling of wellness. It's estimated that the average adult should be drinking between 2.7 litres and 3.7 litres of water per day,[11] a feat that most people fail to achieve even at home. Start your day with a litre of water first thing and always take water with you when you go out. Never forget to check whether or not the tap water is safe to drink where you're travelling and reach for bottled water or a water purification system to safely stay hydrated if the local water isn't potable. Refer to your *home* country's travel recommendations for water safety and never to those of the country you're visiting. Many countries have water that's potable for locals but is different enough to make travellers sick.

## Basic infections

From urinary tract infections (UTIs) to ear infections, any issues that you've had at home might occur on the road.

Painful infections that quickly escalate, such as UTIs, will need immediate attention. In some countries, anyone can buy any antibiotics at a pharmacy without a prescription, while other countries will require a visit to a doctor. If you've had recurring problems with any infection, write down what antibiotic treatment you were given at home so that you have an idea of where to start if you have to buy antibiotics on your own abroad. You may be surprised to learn how cultural treatment plans for such basic infections are. Growing up in the US, I received antibiotics many times for sinus infections and similar problems, only to be told by doctors in the Netherlands that those infections almost always go away on their own. Be open to different treatments for familiar problems.

## How to prepare

The countries you visit will have their own healthcare systems, though ideally you will not need to rely on them. It's a mistake to think that you can prepare for all the health problems you'll encounter while travelling, but you should look critically at what is within your control.

### Get a full checkup from your GP and dentist before leaving

If you have health insurance, you should leave no stone unturned when approaching your health before you leave. You've been having problems with your stomach? Visit your GP. You've been wondering whether you have a cavity? Visit your dentist. When you leave, help with non-emergency problems will not always be covered by your travel insurance.

### Document important medical information

Write down any important medical information and keep it with your travel documents. If you're travelling with a friend or partner, make sure they're aware of any allergies, important conditions, etc. so that they can advocate for you if you're unable to advocate for yourself.

### Have neutral expectations

If you associate medicine purely with science, you're mistaken. Medicine is as entwined with culture as it is with any fact-based foundations. Medical experiences abroad are raw and the treatment you receive will *never* resemble the treatment you'd receive at home. The differences may be shocking, from the attitude towards testing and pharmaceuticals to modesty. I was appalled to receive medical treatment in a Dutch hospital where gowns were not administered and I was expected to walk distances between testing rooms naked. Release any feelings that your home country's cultural approach to health and medicine are the correct or only way. Unless you're willing to travel home for medical treatment, it doesn't matter how things would have been done back home. All that matters is what you have access to now and reacting appropriately.

### *How to react*

The necessary reaction plan to health problems abroad will be determined by the severity of your concerns and the healthcare options at your disposal. If you're having severe problems, you should always seek medical help, no matter the cost. For non-emergency issues, initiate health maintenance mode, which covers these five areas:

1 **Slow down.** When you feel tired, lie down. Go to bed early, even if you don't fall asleep right away. Respond to weakness and fatigue by giving your body the rest it's asking for.

2 **Hydrate.** Keep water by your side and drink continually. If you're losing fluids through diarrhoea or vomiting, this is even more vital. Consider foods with high water content to supplement.

3 **Limit your alcohol intake.** While alcohol is a joy in moderation, it's not good for the body. It's bad for sleep and digestion, which both have an enormous impact on how you feel.

4 **Stay out of the sun.** Extended time in the sun makes you feel tired and your body needs to conserve energy when you're fighting something off.

5 **Eat something nourishing.** Focus on giving your body fuel during times of illness and avoiding greasy and overly processed foods.

If you need to seek medical attention and have some time to prepare, pack a lot of water and snacks. Not all hospitals feed patients while they're waiting. Download the language offline on Google Translate if you're not fluent and use your phone to translate between yourself and the doctor. Try to take someone with you for company and help navigating an unfamiliar system. Solo travellers can look to hostel-goers for company or even their Airbnb host or a staff member from the hotel. Consider asking for advice from people and see if any candidates emerge. A simple 'I need to find a doctor but I'm scared to go alone' can solicit volunteers. Without the normal support system that you'd have at home, you'll have to rely on the people around you. You may come up empty-handed or you may be surprised at how strangers rise to the occasion to help.

On her 30th birthday, travel blogger Lynne Lessard got food poisoning while alone in the Philippines. She hailed a ride to a local hospital where she ultimately needed to be admitted for medical treatment. When they wouldn't admit her without an emergency contact, an unlikely but happy-to-help volunteer emerged: her taxi (or rather, motorized tricycle) driver. 'While I'd rather not have terrible things happen, it's really incredible to see what we're capable of and how other people help,' she said. Another surprise: as it was her birthday, the hospital refused to charge her and gave her medical treatment for free.

Communicating health problems abroad with your team is a little less black and white than communicating tech problems. If you're employed by a company, the country where the company is registered will have laws around workers and health. Since many digital nomads are contract workers or self-employed, sick days are less clear and communication is left to be dealt with on a case-by-case basis.

Sick days that don't affect your team don't need to be communicated. A digital nomad who's ahead of schedule is much less likely to need to notify their team of illness or injury. But if you do find yourself in that situation, highlight your proactivity organization and problem solving, just as with the tech problem response.

## Crime abroad

A bus dropped Bert-Jan off in a border town on the edge of Peru and Ecuador and he needed to orient himself with his *Lonely Planet*. Doing so in the street is the equivalent of holding up a sign that says 'I'm not from here and I'm lost', so he sat down at a restaurant to make a plan over lunch. A man approached and on seeing the guidebook introduced himself as a travelling missionary from El Salvador. The two jumped into stories of travel and they started comparing their plans for Ecuador. Bert-Jan asked him, 'Do you know the best area to cross the border here?' Whether or not they actually *are* unsafe, border towns can often feel like the most precarious parts of any country.

'You look poor and strong, so you'll be fine,' the missionary said nonchalantly. 'The people who want to rob you have tourists all day to choose from; they'll choose someone who looks more worth their time to steal from.' Years later while travelling in Colombia, this mentality was given a name. Colombians have a saying: *dar papaya*. Directly translated as 'to give papaya', it means you shouldn't make it easy for people to take advantage of you. Carrying your camera round your neck, walking around with your phone out or wearing a smartwatch all make it clear that you have something worth stealing.

While no tourist wants to encounter crime, the crime-avoidance stakes are higher for digital nomads. So much more is at risk than vacation memories – the fate of your job or business is directly tied to your ability to open up your laptop and work. Remote workers stay abroad longer carrying ample technology that they rely on heavily for day-to-day life. Here's how to protect your lifestyle.

### How to prepare

No one ever deserves to be a target of crime, but it is everyone's hope that they can avoid brush-ups with it, whether it be violent crime or petty theft and money scams. Travellers should look at what steps they can take to reduce the odds of encountering these situations.

It's highly unlikely that crime will have an enormous effect on your travels, but a crime-avoidance mindset must become a part of your daily life. The amount of precaution you need to exercise will vary wildly between countries and these safety tips are not necessary for all destinations, but it's better to be over-prepared than under-prepared. Here's some common street sense to help you avoid problems.

## Research warnings by country and region

If your country has an up-to-date global travel resource for citizens, consult it when planning *and* leaving for your trip. Be sure to zoom in on the region that you'll be travelling to within each country. Also research common scams specific to the countries you'll be visiting.

## Learn some of the local languages

A lot of scams and petty crimes are circumstantial and being able to handle basic communication can help you avoid such scenarios. Some language skills position you as someone who's less disoriented and more prepared and this helps you be perceived as a more self-assured traveller. You're also able to connect with and receive advice from locals. A traveller once told me that after a nice bout of small talk in a taxi, the cab driver told them, 'Give me a hug when you get out so the people here think you're my friend and won't try to pickpocket you.' The doors to these moments are opened by a shared language.

## Don't buy travel gear that looks unnecessarily expensive

A suitcase with 'Calvin Klein' on the side sends a message that you don't want to broadcast. So does showing train or bus tickets on your iPad or openly wearing a smartwatch in countries with less access to breaking technology. Keep frilly displays to an absolute minimum.

## Document important information

Make a plan for what would happen if your wallet was lost or stolen. You would need to cancel your credit cards, get a replacement passport, etc. Write down your credit card numbers, make digital scans of your passport and have extra copies of everything important.

## Avoid boisterous crowds

It doesn't matter if crowds are happy or angry: don't spend time in a mob. Leave the immediate area right away if a large group suddenly forms. This goes for one-off events like pro-tests as well as sports crowds, which often involve large amounts of alcohol.

### *How to react*

The bus arrived at 4.45 am in Serbia. The bus terminal, like many I'd seen before, was not overtly dangerous, but it made me feel very aware of my surroundings. People were sleeping on the pavement, the bathrooms were very neglected and the people waiting on benches tracked us with their eyes as we walked. Shocked to see a cafe open so early, we quickly hustled through the door to get out of the cold. The air was thick with smoke and full of middle-aged men who turned in unison to watch us. If this had been a movie, the music would have abruptly cut off and you'd have heard the cups clink against the table. Most of the men were smoking cigarettes and drinking coffee, and many were also sipping some clear beverage out of a small shot glass. The attention of every patron was on us, which was in no way dangerous. But it did sacrifice a traveller's greatest asset: discretion.

While always the goal, discretion is not always achievable. Based on height alone, Bert-Jan and I can often be spotted as tourists (and from a distance, at that). Children have run up and asked for pictures with us; adults have pulled out their phones and taken photos *of* us, without asking.

Similarly, Zoe Ashbridge told me stories from when she and her partner were cycling around the world on fitted-out bicycles complete with bright yellow panniers carrying all their belongings. Discretion was impossible, as they attracted curious looks even while cycling around the Scottish Highlands where they lived. One day in Malaysia, they literally turned heads: a driver overtook them on their bikes, his curious stare lingering so long as he passed that he crashed into a parked car. Travellers will become familiar with unexpected attention, most of it harmless, though the feeling of being safe or unsafe is often a grey space.

The world is not made up of strictly safe and unsafe spaces. Safety is a spectrum and an enormous amount of it is a feeling of perceived security. On one end of the spectrum is 'this place looks different from what I'm used to', which is not necessarily the same as 'this place *feels* dodgy', but the two can be easily confused. Next is 'this place *is* dodgy' and finally 'this place is unsafe and I should leave'.

When you feel nervous, take these steps:

- Put technology (laptop, phone, charging cords, etc.) out of sight.
- Don't have any 'loose' belongings: close all bags and empty or zip up pockets.
- Put wallet away and don't show any money.
- Don't distract yourself with headphones, a book or anything else: show that you're paying attention to your surroundings.
- Move to well-lit or well-trafficked areas.
- Find another person or another group to sit or walk with.
- Leave the area.

Here's some common street sense that should be applied while abroad.

## Beware of free things that are offered unsolicited

It's not uncommon for people to volunteer information, directions, etc. and then demand money afterwards. For example, if you're looking around at where to go and some-one eagerly jumps up and volunteers to give you directions, there's a good chance they're going to demand money after delivering that information. Always remember that 'no' is a complete sentence – you can reject any offer with a smile and a 'no, thank you' without having to explain yourself.

## Don't take free alcohol

Person A offering free alcohol as a gesture of hospitality is (not always, but sometimes) an attempt to distract you while Person B pickpockets you. Say no thank you and keep walking.

### Take cues from locals

Pay attention to the way locals behave when trying to gauge safety. Many areas are safe during the day but unsafe at night and you can either avoid those areas after dark or look when locals go inside. If people are gathered in public areas and kids are still playing in the streets, you can take that as a sign that the area is safe.

### Avoid looking lost

Looking lost translates to looking vulnerable. Even if you're not sure you're going in the right direction, carry yourself at a brisk pace with confidence. Be aware of your surroundings and project a confident and self-assured demeanour.

### Be discreet and don't look worth robbing

Beyond not 'giving papaya', travellers shouldn't walk around following Google Maps on their phone. It's more discreet to check your phone briefly and then put it out of sight as you walk. Sometimes for directions or finding travel amenities, *Lonely Planet* is more resourceful than Google, but it attracts attention to walk around carrying it. Pull out guidebooks with discretion.

### Lie if people ask questions and you feel nervous

You don't owe anyone the truth about where you're going or who you're going with. If someone starts asking questions about your plans and it feels suspicious, lie: you're travelling with your brother, a friend is going to meet you any minute, you're married, you're visiting family in the area. Never feel obliged to tell the truth.

## Protect your belongings from everyone

Petty crime happens on the streets, but it also happens in hostels and hotels. Always lock up your belongings at hostels and keep cash scattered between your bags so it's not possible to steal all your money in one swipe. While at a hostel in Nicaragua, I made the mistake of leaving my bags unlocked while I ran out of the room for a few minutes. By the time I came back into the room, the equivalent of $400 had been stolen out of my wallet. I allowed this to happen by keeping all my cash together in one place and failing to lock my bag.

## Never go without cash

Bathrooms, unexpected fees (or bribes), broken ATMs – it's irresponsible to run out of cash. Also avoid ending up with cash that won't be accepted, such as extremely large notes. ATMs will often give you large notes that local restaurants and grocery stores will refuse to accept. If you receive large notes, make a point of breaking them right away or your money might be refused. Spread your cash between bags so that if one of your bags gets lost or stolen, you won't lose everything.

## Buddy up with someone else

Individual swindlers are much less interested in approaching pairs or groups of people. If you ever feel unsafe walking somewhere but aren't able to turn round and go back, see if there's someone else to walk with. Simply ask, 'Do you mind if we walk together?'

### Separate from people who make you uncomfortable

If you feel as though a person or group is following you too closely, separate from them. Cross the street, bend down to tie your shoes and let them pass or go into the next shop or restaurant.

### Pay to feel safe

No amount of money is worth your feeling of safety. If possible, have backup funds or a credit card so that you can pay for a taxi ride or a nice hotel room on the spot. Never let your funds get so low that you don't have the option to feel safe anymore.

### Go with your gut

There's nothing wrong with taking the *next* taxi, taking a detour or refusing help from a local. Your gut should always decide and you don't need to justify it.

### Pass the Headline Test

My personal philosophy while travelling boils down to something I've named *the Headline Test*. If a situation has a negative outcome, would I be embarrassed for my friends and family to read a headline describing it? If the answer is yes, then I'm taking too big a risk. For example, I once slept in a bed that had rat faeces on it because I was too cheap to pay \$2 more for a hostel down the road. I brushed the faeces off, had a terrible night's sleep and was fine. But if I'd fallen sick, that headline would have read: 'Woman With Enough Money For Clean Bed Chose To Sleep In Bed With Rat Faeces On It, Contracts Infectious Disease.' Foreshadow your decisions before you make them.

## Crime

While crime is thought of as the number one risk of travelling, I put it last on this list because it's the least likely thing to disrupt your trip. Travel, like riding in a car, has inherent risks, but they're not that different from the risks you run at home. Computer issues, colds and stomach bugs are much more likely to disrupt your journey. They're all par for the course of travel.

# Par for the course

After weeks of itchiness that wouldn't cease, a doctor looked at my rashy armpits and said one of the most disgusting words in the English language: scabies. My mouth shot open like the guy from *The Scream* painting. 'Like, fleas for humans?' I've never felt mentally slower processing a single word before. She laughed. We had been talking about travel during the examination and she said something that was surprisingly comforting: 'Your first parasite! You're a real traveller now.' Those words echoed around my mind as I processed them. For a moment I felt seasoned, and then I went immediately back to feeling disgusting.

Not a single story in this book has started with things going the right way. Every travel story starts the same: with something going sideways. It's part of the adventure. Normal life throws parking tickets, ripped trousers and lost credit cards at you all the time. You're still driving down life's same potholed highway no matter where you are in the world. It's not something to try to avoid, but rather to prepare for and handle with a good sense of humour. When things go wrong, and they will, remember that disastrous days are par for life's course and the travel ones end up being good bar stories in the end. Promise to tell me your most embarrassing one if we ever cross paths (and I hope we do).

# 07
# Digital nomadism: a lifestyle or a phase?

It was Christmas morning in the Netherlands, but it wasn't a Christmas I recognized. Outside it was damp and grey. The sparkling decorations, trays of divine cut-out cookies, smell of ham in the oven, house packed with family and otherwise *over-the-topness* of American Christmas was nowhere to be found. I went to church where Bert-Jan was playing in the band, and I was relieved to see a familiar face coming towards me to say Hi: one of Bert-Jan's bandmates. I excitedly went in for what I thought was a hug, while he was coming in to give me the kind but very uncomfortable Dutch greeting of three kisses on the cheeks. In my enthusiasm, I forgot about the kiss custom and leaned all the way in. He couldn't brake fast enough to react to my surprise move and we collided in the most uncomfortable greeting of my life: a confused kiss on the neck. My breath stopped with shock and I was burning with embarrassment. If it was possible to die from discomfort, my soul would have left my body.

I would have paid a million dollars to be teleported back to the US at that moment. I longed for a place where I understood the right way to act, always knew what was being said and valued what was happening. Being immersed in another culture had lost all its shine. The past version of myself that thought literally any experience abroad was thrilling and would somehow make me a better person was completely lost in my rear-view mirror. And at that mortifying moment, it didn't feel like growth, experience or anything else I could put a positive spin on. It felt like maybe the fun abroad had run its course.

## Moving past first impressions

Life abroad and I were no longer casual; we were in a deeply committed relationship. Not one I was excelling at, clearly, but one that had decisively left the honeymoon phase. Despite its discomfort, moments like this signal a radically important aspect of life abroad: moving past first impressions.

I've been accused of describing this lifestyle in a negative way. *Me, the remote work enthusiast.* This accusation used to feel like an indictment of my romance with remote work. I think that the conversation about the digital nomad lifestyle has been unbalanced for so long that hearing about any disadvantages comes as a surprise. It's kind of like looking at a picture of the summit of Mount Everest and thinking, '*That's what climbing Everest is like.*' The beauty, magic and grandeur are real and waiting to be discovered; it's just not representative of the entire trek. The digital nomad mystique that makes its way to the mainstream consciousness is only representative of moments, and make no mistake, those moments are real and as magnificent as they seem, but they are just individual steps on the journey.

The odd '*I became a digital nomad and it ruined my life*' clickbait article floats by me on the internet and when I read them, I'm always shocked by just how ill prepared some people were. Be conscious as you consume information online for this reason and remember that not everyone documenting this lifestyle has moved past their first impression of it. Not everyone has missed their first funeral or found themselves in a hospital alone where they have no one there for them but Google Translate. Just as a gap year abroad can never represent the experience of leaving your home country forever, a few months as a digital nomad can never represent the effects of choosing long-term travel over the comforts and conveniences of home.

This lifestyle isn't an escape from reality, it's just life, with all its day-to-day ups and downs. You're still driving down life's same potholed highway no matter where you are in the world, but I personally think that for travellers abroad, that path comes with higher peaks. You might never move past your first impressions of this lifestyle. Should you try digital nomadism for a few weeks, months or even as a working gap year, it's entirely possible that the warnings I've shared will echo like ghost stories against your untarnished experience. If that's the case, I'll be thrilled for you. Maybe you can teach me your secrets of how you avoid problems and embarrassing moments, *a skill I've yet to master.*

If you travel long enough, you'll have to handle all manner of life events abroad. I hope that if the day comes that you experience a toothache or a broken laptop, you'll be emotionally braced because you knew going into this lifestyle that it wasn't a non-stop vacation. That image fuels our daydreams, but it doesn't do you any favours to believe it's achievable on the road.

It's impossible to live in escapism mode and you wouldn't want to because you're building a life that you actively want to experience. No one can crawl into the Instagram grid of a travel influencer and make those curated moments their full-time reality. No one, no matter their budget or work schedule, visits postcard-worthy travel highlights every single day. And even if you *are* jumping from highlight to highlight, they won't all be World Wonders. In Split, Croatia, I visited a local tourist attraction that was just a stray cat. It was a long-furred white cat that napped every day in the same spot, listed jokingly on Google Maps as a tourist attraction. Reviews range from 'distinguished local' to 'he tried to bite me'.

This realization is not a downer: this reality check is your friend. And as your friend who works online and travels, I want you to be prepared because the downsides of this lifestyle slap extra hard when you're not expecting them. As you're reeling from the sting, you're going to find yourself wondering: am I cut out for this at all?

## Getting exactly what you want

This lifestyle isn't a 12-course meal that you're obligated to eat all of out of respect. It's a buffet where you can create a meal that works for you. And learning to unapologetically edit your day to day is going to change your experience radically.

It's important to get what you want out of the digital nomad lifestyle. Frankly I think this statement rings true for every lifestyle, but this is more pressing than in most areas. Why? Because it's a lot of work. Constantly counting how many days are left on your visa, checking flight prices, trying to decipher foreign food labels in shops: while the stimulation is the very thing that you craved back at your desk, it's also exhausting to constantly be reconfiguring. The sheer amount of time I've spent finding bathrooms in my life is probably monstrous. Between visas and language barriers, sometimes you just long for a home life where you get to focus on seeing friends or keeping a fitness schedule. The mental obstacle course burns far more calories than the average day spent going to work in the same place, at roughly the same time, with the same people.

## How to constantly edit

We'd been travelling for months, me with the remnants of my normal life in my parents' basement in the US and Bert-Jan with an apartment being sublet in the Netherlands. Inside a private hostel room in Cusco, Peru, we sat on the bed deep in conversation until late morning, not drawn out into the common areas, not lured out by the idea of Cusco waiting beyond our door. We were steeped in a cloud of daydreams, the same as many times before, except our daydreams had changed. Talks of joining sailing crews and living in vans had recessed like the tide, unearthing new topics of herb gardens and apartment decor. We wanted to stop travelling. Not forever, but decisively for now. It had a slight air of sadness, seeing the page close on an exciting chapter of life, but that air was blown away by a gust of excitement for what was next.

Life's pendulum will always swing both ways. It would be madness to try to stop it.

The beginning of a great trip feels like sitting in sweltering heat, drinking in the humid air, dreaming of relief. Then finally, you jump into cold blue waters. It's delicious; you feel the contrast with your whole body. You're engulfed in the reality of your plans coming to fruition.

It's a high that digital nomads keep chasing because we never leave those blue waters. Not for a long time, at least. We don't take a dip once a year on vacation and then return home to pine until the next year. It's easy to forget what that change even feels like. Raised adrenaline levels, overall higher happiness level, whatever the cause, it's often rooted more in contrast and flexibility than in travel itself.

'The conversation is much richer, much deeper and more nuanced than just travelling,' said Mitko Karshovski, founder of the *Work From Mars* newsletter. 'Flexibility is the true underlying theme.'

It was in 2016 that Mitko and his wife first tested the remote work lifestyle on a three-month trial trip to Bulgaria. They liked it so much that in 2017 they packed up their lives in Ohio and became fully nomadic and they've been drifting in and out of full-time travel ever since. 'Only a small, aggressive percentage of the remote workers will travel full-time forever. Most people naturally go between seasons of life.'

When you experience travel fatigue, burnout and imbalance, seek contrast in your life by adjusting these factors of your lifestyle.

### Speed

With a slower speed of travel comes less feverish activity. A constant cycle of packing and unpacking, searching for the nearest food store and so on is a routine that has you constantly deciphering your surroundings. See whether there's comfort in returning to the same cafe or bar every Friday, developing a routine, staying somewhere long enough to make habits and even build real friendships.

### Community

While you could say that the opportunity of remote work has radically improved since Steven K Roberts set off in 1983 (who doesn't prefer high-speed WiFi over a payphone and an acoustic coupler?), the glue that holds the community together is less certain. Steven counted on micro-communities – cyclists, ham radio operators, one nationwide fraternity – for support and occasional housing to relieve the chain of camping. He also invited strangers out to cycle with him, which he referred to as his Call to Nomadness.[12] Now, despite the constant digital connection, loneliness is a chief complaint about the lifestyle.

Seek out community when loneliness starts to take a toll on you: online, locally or both. Keep strong bonds with your existing community back home, schedule weekly or fortnightly video calls. To find friends locally who are also in the digital nomad community, consider a hostel (dorm room or private room) or a co-living space. Consider going to a popular digital nomad destination in search of friendships.

## Climate

Consider a more extreme climate, whether it's hot or cold. Along with more extreme temperatures, you'll find different foods and local customs to explore.

## Accommodation

Is your accommodation meeting your current needs? These needs will change over time. There's a radical difference between the experience of living in an apartment in New York City and in a fjord house in Norway. Noise levels, population density and overall intensity have a huge impact on your mood that can be invisible but very influential. Someone who's been living in hostels may benefit from some alone time in an Airbnb and someone who's been living alone could see a huge difference in energy levels by surrounding themselves with hostel-goers.

### Work–life balance

Specifically, I recommend you look at your work–*fun* balance. Take stock of how much fun you're having day to day or week to week and adjust immediately until you find balance.

### Work type

There's no escaping the need to work, but when you find yourself constantly overwhelmed by stress or unmotivated, explore new opportunities. Evaluate when it's time for a new job, a supplemental side hustle, going full-time self-employed or even pursuing a 6- or 12-month contract of local work to offer a break from the online world.

### Goals

Instead of chasing sunrise hikes and bucket list vistas, try on new goals. Give yourself what you need: set a 30-day goal of prioritizing reading, movement, socialization and so on every day and see if your mental health and mood improve.

### Ease

Seek a more convenient country or accommodation. Simply relocating to a destination where you speak the language will offer a strong feeling of ease. If you have someone close in your life who you enjoy staying with, ask if you can spend two weeks or a month with them. A staycation with a loved one can be an incredible opportunity to recharge your batteries.

Sipping a cold beer in a hostel in Costa Rica, I overheard a woman doing a video interview for a job as an English teacher for an international school. Her questions started out covering the basics like safety, but then she proceeded to ask things I'd never even thought of before: how reliable was the electrical infrastructure and how often did the roads wash away and become impassable in the rainy season? When her call was over, another backpacker who had also been eavesdropping asked the question we were all thinking: 'Are you really thinking of moving there?' The spectrum of ease is wide and when travel burnout sets in, it's often time to assess where you're at on that scale.

No one operates like a satellite that gets programmed, launched onto its path in space and left to orbit. We're much more like sailboats, constantly adjusting to the wind and tides, reacting to everything around us – things both in and out of our control. Pull into a harbour. Check the map. Adjust your course. You were never meant to stick to the original plan forever and things might change in surprising ways.

## Five months versus five years

Should you travel as a remote worker for five months, I can take a guess at what your life will look like. The process of planning and executing a huge life change will have altered the way you see the world. Your perception of what's possible will be shaped like a pebble by the waterfall of every new destination, sudden friendship, each problem solved and once-in-a-lifetime experiences. While you'll have a much deeper understanding of when you're most productive, you'll probably still be figuring out work–life integrations. Any persistent self-sabotaging habits, like procrastination and disorganization, will have taken their toll on your mental health and professional relationships. You'll be more adaptable but also more sensitive to missed moments back home, both big and small. The pains of longing for your favourite foods, old friends and familiar surroundings will begin to set in. Five months of digital nomadism looks very different than five years.

If you stay a digital nomad for five years, your life will look different. You'll have travelled to countless dream destinations and some truly surprising countries. After five years abroad, your friendships will have changed. Your network will still include some friends at home, but they'll have embarked on new life chapters and people who also spend their time abroad will make up a large part of your circle. You might not have found the job that's 'the one', but your income will probably have stabilized and your professional network will be strong.

Travelling, once a hectic activity, will be second nature. You will know how to do it, what to expect, and will have seen how things can go wrong. Thought-out systems will silently structure the way you work and handle your physical belongings. There will be less anxiety from the uncertainty and maybe just less uncertainty to start with. Uncertainty, a part of the human condition, can never be outgrown, but after doing things over and over like visas and border crossings, you'll have clear expectations of how things normally go. The five-year mark of digital nomadism isn't a milestone most remote workers will cross because most people will have followed different paths.

## Changing gears and common paths

'When will you stop travelling?' It was a fair question and one I got a lot from my friends, family and colleagues alike in 2017 when I first set sail. Depending on my mood, I would either quickly summarize my travel plans and say they were open-ended or share how I really felt: 'I want to be a leaf in the world and go wherever life blows me.' The sadness I felt at leaving Chicago and leaving my family was impossible to put into words, but I felt like life was taking me in a different direction; I wanted to jump into the currents of life and find out where it went. One month into my travels, Bert-Jan blew into my life and along with him the surprise of moving to the Netherlands.

Back then, I never could have dreamt that my online work would give me so much. The road of remote work has taken me to unexpected places and created incredible opportunities, though the path has come with many forks along the way and it hasn't always been clear what's up next.

Digital nomads with a home base waiting for them will have a clear path back to normality: go back home whenever mood, health, family responsibilities or financial constraints dictate it. Those who give up their homes and are flexible about which city or country they live in next are faced with an intimidating number of options. Here are some common paths that digital nomads take.

- **Citizen seeker:** Those who find countries and cultures that they love can seek pathways to immigration, with the end goal of permanent residency or naturalized citizenship.

- **Serial expat:** Move from *digital nomad* to *expat* by using long-stay visas, work visas or residency visas to stay in a country for years, but always with the expectation of moving onto somewhere new eventually. The people who move from country to country every few years often call themselves serial expats.

- **The lover:** This may lead you to stay where you're at or travel somewhere new. If your partner has a job that requires travel and you decide to follow them, you'd be referred to as a trailing spouse.

- **Chronic adventurer:** When your current type of travel becomes tiresome, reach for a new medium. If travel hasn't lost its magic but you need a new experience, try something new like backpacking, bikepacking, living in a campervan, group travel or sailing. This was the path that Steven K Roberts took when he mounted the *Winnebiko* for the first time in 1983.

## The digital nomad movement

*'If you think too much about where you're going, you lose respect for where you are.'*[13]    STEVEN K ROBERTS

Steven K Roberts was sipping a cup of orange juice at a roadside fruit stand in Florida. It was his first day back on his bike after briefly hitchhiking on a sailboat through the Florida Keys, a chain of scenic tropical islands in the US. For the first time in a while, he was alone; that was until a group of cyclists appeared off in the distance. Steven watched as they purposefully approached and ground to a halt at the juice stand. They carried bags on their bikes, signalling that they weren't just hobbyists out for the day, but Steven couldn't quite place them. They were kitted out in expensive-looking gear and had an air of intensity that seemed out of place with bicycle life that Steven had come to know after 3,500 miles on the road. Curious, Steven asked them about their travels.

'We're gonna see the Pacific Ocean on August 17th. What about you?' they shot back with a surprising air of competition. Steven replied that he'd probably make it to the Pacific, but he didn't anticipate that happening until sometime the next year. Unimpressed, the cyclists boasted their plan: they had drawn a straight line across the US and were going to complete their ocean-to-ocean voyage as quickly as possible. *'August 17th?'* Steven circled back to their initial statement. 'What if you want to climb a mountain? Or you fall in love?' Steven grasped at straws, trying to understand this alien species. 'I don't know what your trip is man, but we're going to see the Pacific Ocean on the 17th,' they said as they chugged their juice and zipped off, leaving a dust cloud in their wake.

Steven's journey had never been about the destination, and it had even stopped being about the technology somewhere after the first few thousand miles. His journey to compute his way across America started out as a tech challenge and an attempt to construct a lifestyle entirely of passions. Along the way it morphed into a normal, happy life that happened to be lived on a bicycle and in a tent. The cycling chapter of life lasted about a decade. When it was time for something new, life on water replaced life on a bike. Over the years, he's explored iterations of his aquatic dream, including high-tech sea kayaking and micro-trimarans (small sailboats). At the time of writing, Steven was living on a 50-foot power boat while he was finessing his new mobile digitizing lab on land during the day. A lot has changed since he became the first digital nomad in 1983, but he's still living a life constructed entirely out of passions.

Rob Palmer (digital nomad circa 1999) is working online and living in Thailand, while travelling often for family and fun. Nic Bartlett (circa 2007) works remotely between Kraków in Poland and the US with his partner, still happily working for the same company that he's been with for more than a decade. Travis and Heather Sherry (circa 2012) are still location independent and travel often with their two kids, in addition to working in real estate. Rachel and Sasha Story (circa 2016) are still fully nomadic and splitting their time between adventuring abroad and being with loved ones in the US. Mitko Karshovski (circa 2016) and his wife have settled into a home base in Ohio and are enjoying the sensation of growing roots in their local community while still travelling often for fun. Gabe Marusca (circa 2019) is slowly and blissfully travelling around Asia, Europe and Latin America while diversifying his online business. Krystal and Eric Nagle (circa 2021) are still enjoying corporate life, now out of a custom-built van parked somewhere beautiful in the US. Bert-Jan and I (circa 2017) are travelling from country to country looking for a place that feels like home.

As you look back over the experiences of remote workers from over the decades, the technical catalytic moments of digital nomadism are easy to spot: portable computers, home internet, internet cafes and WiFi have changed the landscape of work forever. The pandemic marked an unexpected milestone in the way society sees remote work, finally boosting its cultural cachet. Social distancing and government shutdowns accelerated the public image and acceptance of remote work in a way that specialists will probably be analysing for decades to come. Technologically, we've been there for years; culturally, society needed time to catch up.

I don't need to rattle off statistics about the explosion of remote work to illustrate the viability, validity and longevity of this movement. The gig has been up for a long time: sitting at the same desk for 2,000 hours a year is not the *only* acceptable way for workers to spend their finite amount of time. I expect the remote work movement to grow exceptionally, but you won't find me trying to convince anyone not interested in its gifts. I smile when naysayers grumble about digital nomadism sounding too good to be true and that their desk job could never possibly be done as effectively from a beach somewhere. Maybe they're right or maybe they're just afraid of the change. What they fail to realize is: we're not coming for their jobs, we're just leaving with ours.

## The real gift of remote work

*Amor fati*: the love of one's fate.

I was at a crossroads in life, again, slowly walking around a market full of handmade goods back in Chicago where it all started. I didn't browse to shop, the market was just a distraction from my debate about which turn to take next. Weighing choices was a constant internal monologue that I needed a break from, so I walked through rows and rows of colourful distracting goods and smiling vendors, letting my mind churn through possible plans in the background. Reminding myself that I really shouldn't buy anything, a small pink-orange badge caught my heart. My eyes lingered long at its white letters reading 'Do your best'. I slowly picked it up and ran my fingers over its simple message and reflected on how much had changed.

It was only a few months before that in this same city that I had plastered my life with messages about overcoming fear, chasing dreams and being who I really wanted to be. Those messages quietly faded from the walls of my mind with every step forward, successful freelance project executed and problem solved. New reminders have become resident in my mind: Do your best. Figure it out. Fight for life's Plan A. It's worth it.

These mantras originally reminded me to go after the big things in life: the flashy, scrapbook-worthy moments. Even more so now they remind me to focus on the small things. When I reach back through the cherished moments that working online has given me, it's the unexpected pictures that are the most vivid. While I am privileged to have memories of swimming through crystal-clear blue ocean waters, walking centuries-old cobblestone streets and seeing some of the Wonders of the World, those aren't the most important souvenirs in my memory bank.

The memories that shine the brightest are moments I never could have anticipated from this journey: being a birth partner for my best friend who became a single mother to twins, the satisfaction of realizing that I'd made it as an entrepreneur and spending more time with Bert-Jan than I ever could have done while working nine to five in an office. I have been able to use my finite amount of time in a radically different way as a result of working online.

Should you choose to forgo Monday to Friday for yesterday, today and tomorrow, your interpretation of what's possible will never be the same. You will find yourself in unexpected places, surrounded by unexpected people, solving unexpected problems. The ability to say yes to so many of life's invitations will be one of the great adventures of your life. I'm so excited for you.

# Notes

## Introduction

1 J Pham. 'Technomad: Remote working to fuel your travels', *Oi Vietnam*, 1 April 2015. https://issuu.com/oivietnam/docs/oi_april_2015_web (archived at https://perma.cc/3H7W-PM3X)
2 S K Roberts. Digital nomad FAQ, Nomadic Research Labs, 1985. https://microship.com/digital-nomad-faq-1985 (archived at https://perma.cc/PSJ8-UH4L)
3 S K Roberts. Tidal passion, Nomadic Research Labs, 1990. https://microship.com/passion (archived at https://perma.cc/U6JH-TV3Y)

## Chapter 1

4 M Andrew. *Am I There Yet?: The loop-de-loop zig zagging journey to adulthood*, Crows Nest, NSW: Allen & Unwin, 2018

## Chapter 2

5 A H Maslow. A theory of human motivation, *Psychological Review*, 50 (4), 430–437, Washington, DC: American Psychological Association, 1943

# Chapter 3

6 J Clear. *Atomic Habits*, New York: Avery, 2018
7 E J Dickey. *Sleeping with Strangers*, Boston: Dutton, 2007

# Chapter 4

8 S K Roberts (2016) The Roberts law of fractal to-do list complexity, Nomadic Research Labs, 2016. https://microship.com/roberts-law-fractal-list-complexity (archived at https://perma.cc/AX7B-FLEV)
9 M Kondo. *The Life-Changing Magic of Tidying Up: The Japanese art of decluttering and organizing*, Berkeley, CA: Speed Press, 2014

# Chapter 5

10 E T Sullivan. Once worth $3B, online tutoring giant VIPKid will end flagship program in China, Edsurge News, 2021. www.edsurge.com/news/2021-10-20-once-worth-3b-online-tutoring-giant-vipkid-will-end-flagship-program-in-china (archived at https://perma.cc/MC27-ET3R)

# Chapter 6

11 Water: How much should you drink every day?, Mayo Clinic, 2022. www.mayoclinic.org/healthy-lifestyle/nutrition-and-healthy-eating/in-depth/water/art-20044256 (archived at https://perma.cc/5DV7-35QT)

# Chapter 7

**12** S K Roberts. Call to nomadness, Nomadic Research Labs, 1990. https://microship.com/call-to-nomadness (archived at https://perma.cc/9SNW-YKRJ)

**13** S K Roberts. Electronic cottage on wheels, *Whole Earth Review*, Spring 1987. https://microship.com/electronic-cottage-on-wheels-whole-earth-review (archived at https://perma.cc/6NDG-HMN3)

# Index

# Looking for another book?

Explore our award-winning
books from global business
experts in Skills and Careers

Scan the code to browse

www.koganpage.com/sce